# Composed

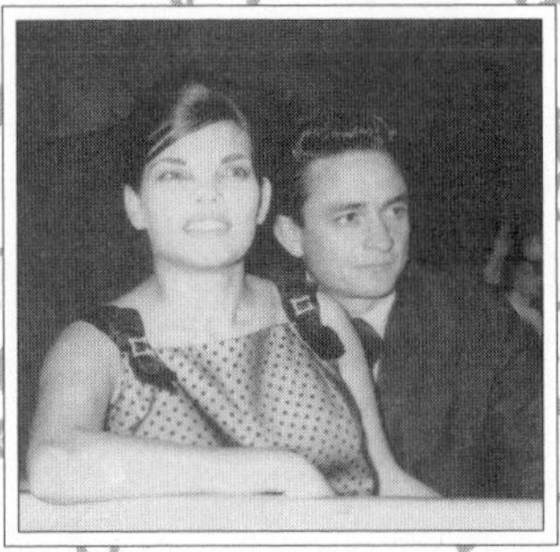
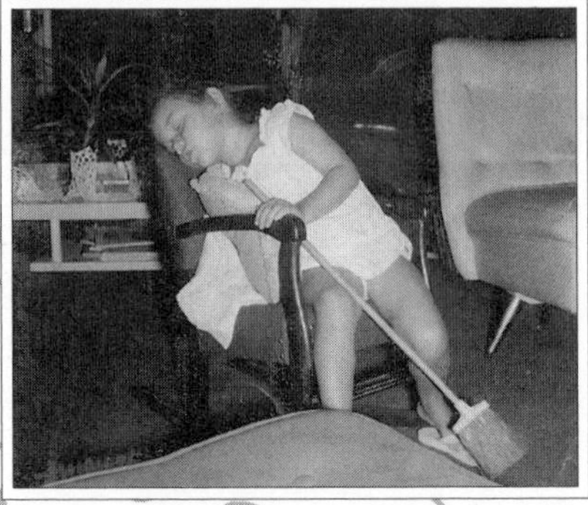
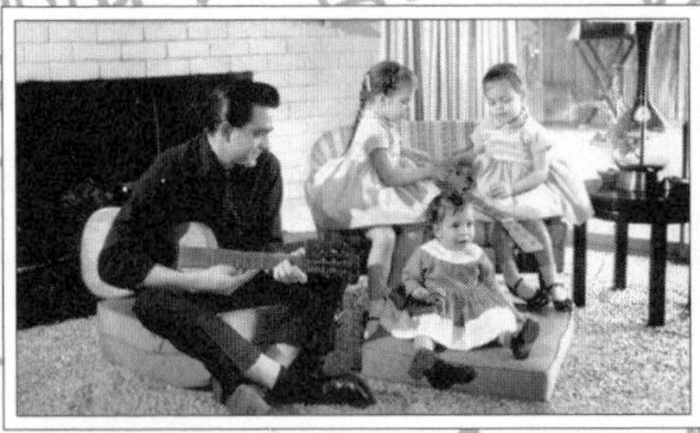
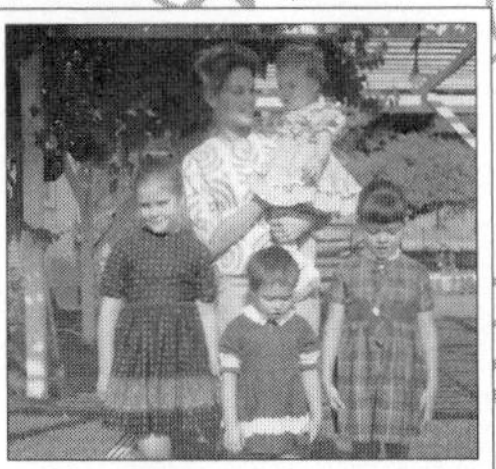
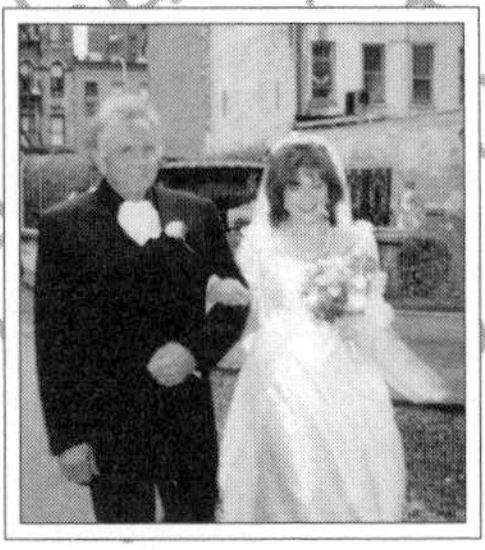
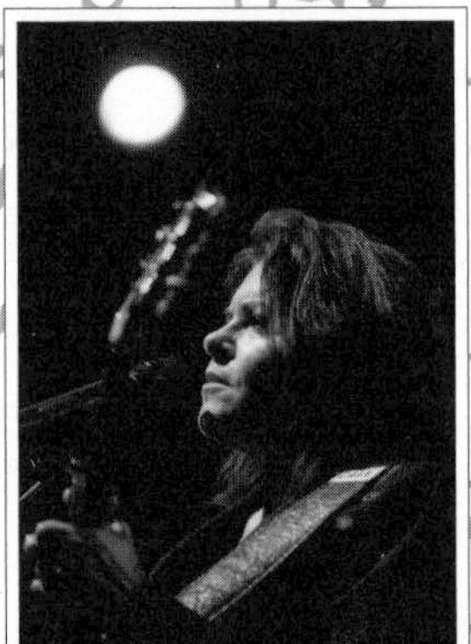
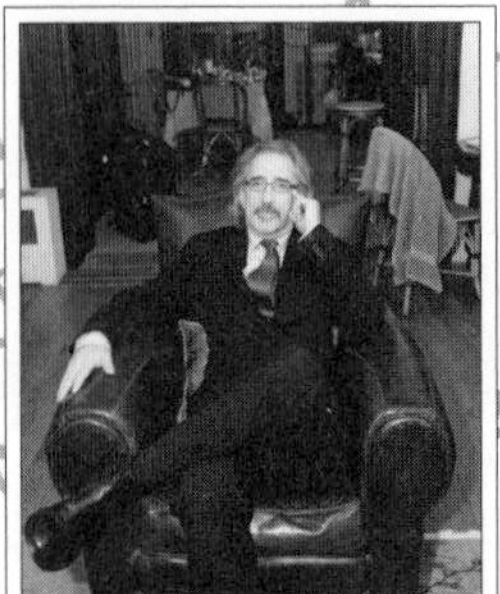
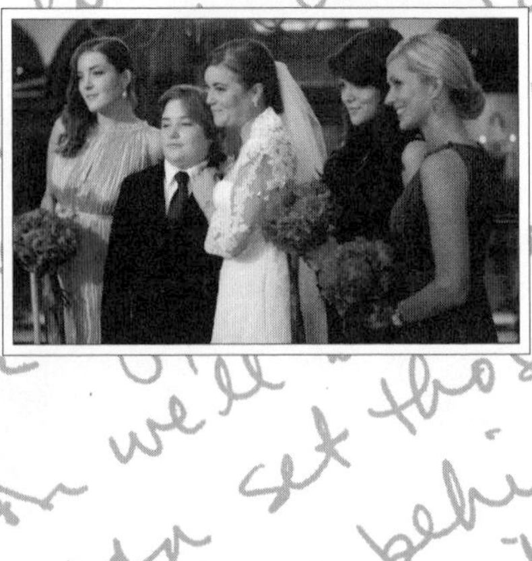
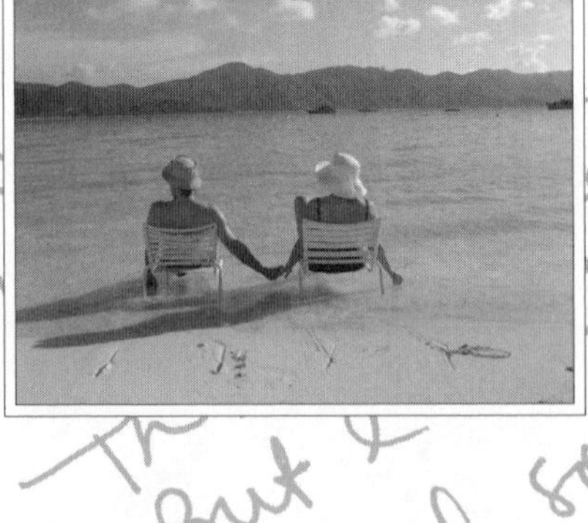

# ROSANNE CASH

# Composed

*a memoir*

VIKING

VIKING

Published by the Penguin Group

Penguin Group (USA) Inc., 375 Hudson Street,
New York, New York 10014, U.S.A.
Penguin Group (Canada), 90 Eglinton Avenue East, Suite 700, Toronto,
Ontario, Canada M4P 2Y3 (a division of Pearson Penguin Canada Inc.)
Penguin Books Ltd, 80 Strand, London WC2R 0RL, England
Penguin Ireland, 25 St Stephen's Green, Dublin 2, Ireland
(a division of Penguin Books Ltd)
Penguin Books Australia Ltd, 250 Camberwell Road, Camberwell,
Victoria 3124, Australia (a division of Pearson Australia Group Pty Ltd)
Penguin Books India Pvt Ltd, 11 Community Centre,
Panchsheel Park, New Delhi–110 017, India
Penguin Group (NZ), 67 Apollo Drive, Rosedale, North Shore 0632,
New Zealand (a division of Pearson New Zealand Ltd)
Penguin Books (South Africa) (Pty) Ltd, 24 Sturdee Avenue,
Rosebank, Johannesburg 2196, South Africa

Penguin Books Ltd, Registered Offices: 80 Strand, London WC2R 0RL, England

First published in 2010 by Viking Penguin, a member of Penguin Group (USA) Inc.

1 3 5 7 9 10 8 6 4 2

Scenes from this memoir were published in different variations in *The Oxford American*,
*Joe* magazine, *The New York Times Magazine*, *Performing Songwriter* magazine, and *Da Capo
Best Music Writing 2000*, edited by Peter Guralnick, published by Da Capo Press.

Excerpt from "An Arundel Tomb" from *Collected Poems* by Philip Larkin. Copyright © 1988,
2003 by the Estate of Philip Larkin. Reprinted by permission of Farrar, Straus and Giroux, LLC.

All photographs from the author's personal collection
Photo of Rosanne Cash with moon in background on page iv: Brad Barket / PictureGroup

LIBRARY OF CONGRESS CATALOGING-IN-PUBLICATION DATA
Cash, Rosanne.
Composed : a memoir / Rosanne Cash.
p. cm.
ISBN 978-0-670-02196-3
1. Cash, Rosanne. 2. Singers—United States—Biography. I. Title.
ML420.C2654A3 2010
782.421642092—dc22
[B]     2010010327

Printed in the United States of America
Set in Warnock Pro
Designed by Francesca Belanger

*For John*

# Composed

# INTRODUCTION

For my entire life I have been trying to give voice to the rhythms and words that underscore, propel, and inform me. Because my peripheral vision is more acute than my direct powers of observation, and my love of an A-minor chord is more charged and refined than my understanding of my own psyche, I have often attempted to explain my experiences to myself through songs: by writing them, singing them, listening to them, deconstructing them, and letting them fill me like food and water. I have charted my life through not only the songs I've composed, but the songs I've discovered, the songs that have been given to me, the songs that are a part of my legacy and ancestry. Through them I've often found meaning, and relief, while at other times I've failed to recognize or understand a rhythm or a theme until it became urgent or ingrained and I finally came across a song that captured the experience.

My life has been circumscribed by music. I have learned more from songs than I ever did from any teacher in school. They are interwoven and have flowed through the most important relationships in my life—with my parents, my husband, and my children. Songs have unfolded in my living room and under the spotlight. For me music has always involved journeys, both literal and metaphoric.

1

Sometimes I took the journey first and found the song waiting at the destination. Some songs have led me to true love. Occasionally a song has been only a faint whisper at the periphery of a larger event, though it was always present. Many of my own songs have taken the long way around, as I circled the edges of an experience, examining the placement of the furniture or the color of the room, the backbeat and the verses, the chord progression and the melody, constantly roaming and constantly curious.

I dream of songs. I dream they fall down through the centuries, from my distant ancestors, and come to me. I dream of lullabies and sea shanties and keening cries and rhythms and stories and backbeats. I dream of the Summer of Love and the British Invasion and the cries of Appalachia and the sound and soul of the Mississippi Delta.

I have resisted, so many times, correcting public misperceptions about me and my life—out of pride, out of pain, or out of a longing for privacy. But I relish the opportunity to write about my life in this book—not to set any record straight, but to extend the poetry, and to find the more subtle melodies and themes in a life that on reflection seems much longer than the years I have lived. Documenting one's life in the midst of living it is a strange pursuit. I have always wanted to live as a beginner, and writing a memoir in some ways defies that notion, but I consider this book as a first installment in an ongoing story. I don't know why some memories have persisted while others have faded, but I trust tenacity, so those are the memories I have written about. This is not a chronological fact-check of my life, and I am sure my sisters or my husband or my children remember some of these events very differently. I have abandoned my reliance on the external facts to support an individual truth, and everyone is entitled to his or her own.

This is mine: So far, so good. More to come. More is always to come.

was born in Memphis, Tennessee, on May 24, 1955, a month before my dad's first single, "Cry, Cry, Cry," was released on Sun Records. My mother had only two dresses that fit her in late pregnancy, she told me, and in her final month, during the most summerlike of the sultry late spring days in East Memphis, she would sit on the steps of the front porch and eat an entire washbasin of cherry tomatoes. It was her one craving. On the afternoon of May 24, my mother went to her regular appointment with her obstetrician, who examined her and told her to go straight to the hospital. "This baby is going to be born today," he said. I was born after only four hours of labor, at eight o'clock that evening. My mother later told me that the loneliest she had ever felt was when she was wheeled through the double doors of the hospital maternity ward to give birth and looked back to see my dad standing forlornly in the waiting room. He paced and smoked there for the next four hours while she labored alone and chewed on a wet washcloth when the pains overtook her; she always spoke with great resentment about the fact that she was given a damp washcloth to suck and then left alone in a hospital room. She was awake for the entire four hours of labor and given nothing for pain, and then put to sleep for the actual birth. It all sounded like a mean-spirited, medieval exercise in physical endurance and emotional isolation. Her accounts of it were so cinematic and full of emotion that I grew up terrified of the prospect of childbirth. I had very few fantasies about having children or being a mother, because I could not get past the specter of childbirth, which seemed almost a horrible end in itself, with something only vague and indefinable on the other side of it. The fact that I eventually did bear four children, delivered both "naturally" and with pain medication, never really lessened my fear.

When my mother went back for her six-week checkup after my birth, the doctor informed her that she was pregnant again. My sister Kathy was born ten months and twenty-three days after me. Kathy was a fragile child who had mysterious illnesses and the worst versions of every childhood disease, and I have always felt guilty that I may have taken all the nutrients out of my mother's body when I inhabited her womb, just before Kathy's arrival there.

Two years after Kathy's birth, my sister Cindy was born, and soon after that we moved from Memphis to Southern California. My sister Tara was born shortly after we settled in Encino, in the San Fernando Valley. My mother's fourth pregnancy and delivery were difficult for her. She carried Tara for ten months and endured a hard sixteen-hour labor. After the birth of her fourth daughter, my mother, in tears, informed my father that she was finished with childbearing, even though she had initially said she wanted six children. My father agreed, although he harbored a secret desire for a son, which he finally got when I was fifteen and he was married to June, not my mother.

My parents bought Johnny Carson's house on Hayvenhurst Avenue in Encino. My most vivid memory of the three years we lived there was of the day a film crew showed up in our living room to tape a show called *Here's Hollywood*. My mother was extremely nervous, and we children were made to dress up in poufy dresses, white ankle socks, and black patent leather shoes, with our hair pulled tightly back into bows. We had to sit absolutely still and silent on the sofa next to my parents while the camera was trained on us and the interviewer spoke to them. Then we were sent outside while Mom and Dad were interviewed alone. The whole experience was profoundly unsettling to me. It may have been the first time that I registered—at age five—how it felt to be truly angry. I didn't like how my mother changed for the camera, showing only a social veneer that didn't represent her true self at all, and I didn't like it that my dad had even allowed them in our house. I recognized the falsity, and silently rebelled against the intrusion. Thus began a lifelong wariness of journalists.

But I loved the house.

It had a pool and a big yard, and the room I shared with my sisters had *Alice in Wonderland* murals on the wall behind the twin beds. We lived on the corner, with a school crossing in front of our house. Every morning and afternoon a crossing guard showed up in her car and waited for the school bus. As it arrived, she got out, slipped her plastic orange neon vest over her clothes, picked up her little stop sign, and positioned herself at the crosswalk to guide the children across the street. This was the most fascinating ritual in the world to me, and the first few times I saw her I ran out to speak to her. She was very kind to me, but after several days, when my mother saw me actually get into the crossing guard's car to talk to her, she forbade me to pay her any more visits. At age four, seriously disappointed and with great longing, I stationed myself in the picture window at the front of the house twice a day to observe her and the children from afar. Part of the romance for me was the older children, for I badly wanted to go to school.

Sensing my frustration, my mother eventually enrolled me in a nursery school down the street for two or three days a week. Although I enjoyed it, I discovered that it didn't provide enough to satisfy my curiosity. I would ask my mother to read me every sign, every paper, every milk carton and package I saw. I insisted she tell me every word and what it meant, nearly driving her crazy in the process, and then I tried to memorize their spellings and meanings. On learning that Europe was a place across the ocean, I asked her if "European" was a real word. She made a joke about going to the bathroom along the lines of "You're peeing" and refused to say whether it was a real word, which made me furious with her. She didn't take my intense need to learn about language seriously, and I was desperate for someone who understood my hunger. My dad would have understood, but he was gone much of the time, and during his recent visits home he had become strange, dark, and intensely distracted. Although I'm not sure why, I didn't go to kindergarten; bored senseless, I began to create imaginary friends, all of whom were adults. Much later in life, a genial psychiatrist to whom I had confided this fact pointed out how unusual it was for a child to have adult imaginary friends, but it still seems perfectly natural to me. I felt safe with them, and they taught me a great deal. I still think of them fondly and I have a deep superstition about speaking their names aloud. They were my own personal crossing guards.

When I was six years old, we moved to Casitas Springs, not far from Ventura and about seventy miles north of Los Angeles. That September I started first grade at the Academy of St. Catherine, which I attended until seventh grade. My sister Kathy began kindergarten there at the same time, and I felt both nervous and superior about being inside the main school building, in real elementary school, while she was in the Quonset hut outside that housed the younger children. I felt a particular sense of responsibility and protection toward her, since she was so much more fragile than me, or so I perceived.

A convent school, the Academy of St. Catherine was a rambling collection of buildings, surrounded by eucalyptus and oak trees and tucked into the base of a hill above Ventura. Boys were allowed to attend up until the sixth grade, and then it was all girls from seventh through twelfth. Even so, there were few boys in the lower grades; thinking back on it now, I can't imagine why the parents of any boy would have sent him to St. Catherine's when he would have been so outnumbered by females. I was taught by conservative, strict nuns, only some of whom were suited to teach children, or even be in the presence of children. I recall only two lay teachers, a Mrs. Husmann who taught third and fourth grades in one big room, and an elderly music instructor who came in once a week for a half hour to warble songs to us. We were required to repeat these tunes back to her, with great reluctance and embarrassment, while the nun who was our regular teacher stood by rigidly at the front of the classroom, ready to yell at whoever wasn't singing.

On the whole I didn't like my teachers and I didn't like the Catholicism that was forced on me in the most punitive and pernicious way possible on a daily basis. I don't remember having attended church or having been exposed to any kind of religion when we lived in Encino, but Casitas Springs was the beginning of the paring down of my life and the curtailing of my internal freedom. A punitive God took up residence in my home and school and mind. At the age of seven I was forced to go to confession every week, and so had to scour my memory for sins and transgressions I might have committed. On one egregious occasion, after a sexually experimental playdate with a little boy who was the son of a friend of my mother's, in the heat of shame and urgency, I confessed adultery to the priest behind the screen in the suffocating little booth, not having a clue what adultery really meant. Believing my account, he kept me in the confessional for nearly half an hour, while my classmates waited impatiently in the chapel outside the door, and castigated me in severe, harsh terms. He gave me penances of multiple rosaries and other long, guilty, sweaty prayers, leaving me terrified and certain that I had been irretrievably damned to hell. I spent years hiding my secret from my mother, who I was certain would punish and humiliate me far worse than the priest if she ever learned the truth.

Not only did the religion I was subjected to as a young child translate all my natural inclinations—sexual and artistic curiosity—into forms of sin, but, even worse, it led me to believe that (my sins notwithstanding) as a Catholic I was someone special, someone blessed, someone who was privy to a true faith, someone who would be welcomed into heaven while others would be cast away. There was a box in my classroom to collect quarters for "pagan babies," the front of which was adorned with a photo of an African baby, whose face I stared at with pity and awe. The entitlement of being Catholic just about ruined me. Thankfully, I am my own pagan baby now, with a bowl of quarters in my kitchen cabinet as a constant reminder that my soul remains unconverted and expansively unredeemed.

I remember myself during this period as a withdrawn, pudgy girl with a swollen face and a foggy head. At the time I thought that the other girls were real girls and that I was some kind of phantom of one, a counterfeit with a strange, hidden life who lived in close proximity to a den of rattlesnakes. That image is not intended as a metaphor; rattlesnakes wandered through our yard on a regular basis.

As a toddler, my little sister Tara once stepped on a baby rattler out in the yard. I was with her, and I saw the snake just as she stepped off it. I knew it was a rattlesnake because the babies were almost translucent. Everyone said the babies were more poisonous than the adults (which turned out not to be true, though I didn't know it at the time), so I picked Tara up, ran into the house, and pulled off her high-topped toddler shoes, examining her feet carefully. No fang marks. Nothing. I was not satisfied, however, and worried for a week that she would fall ill with snakebite poisoning. I stared at her nervously when I came home from school and through the evenings, ever watchful for the unknown but surely telltale signs of sickness. My mother grew adept at killing rattlers in the front yard, some as long as six feet, by attacking them with a garden hoe. After chopping off their heads, she would hurl their bodies like a javelin onto the fence, where they were left to hang.

I ultimately developed a near-psychotic phobia about snakes, which resonates in me even now. After those years of forced rattlesnake immersion, when we left the mountainside I saw only one more snake in my entire childhood: a pet king snake that the boy next door brought over so he could tease me. He didn't anticipate, nor did I, the effect it would have on me, and he stood openmouthed in disbelief as I jumped up onto a table, screaming and crying in hysteria at the sight of it. He looked thoughtful for a moment, then quietly turned around and took it back to his own home. I never again saw a snake, or even mentioned the word, until I moved out at the age of eighteen.

The other menaces on our land (besides the drunken folk singers who regularly wandered to our door looking for salvation and inspiration in the person of Johnny Cash) were giant poisonous desert arachnids, which I would trap in mayonnaise jars as my own private science lab and spider jail. I experimented with them, feeding them and not feeding them, letting them have oxygen and not letting them have oxygen, to see how long they would survive. I had no mercy. A scorpion or a tarantula was a nasty thing to find in your bedroom, and one could easily bite my little sister as she was toddling in the yard, or our mother's Chihuahua. One of them did bite our German shepherd, causing his face to swell horribly. I remember my dad's pity for the dog, and the dog's oblivious expression as he walked around with his face almost double in size. My dad explained that the dog had been bitten on the head, and I corrected him, silently, to myself. *Not the head. The face.* I felt a great sense of power when I entrapped a giant tarantula in a large jar and put my face close to the glass, where it could do nothing to hurt me.

The Chihuahua, for her part, escaped any such attack, but gave birth to four puppies, all of whom died at birth because their poor little slip of a mother had whelped too many at once. My dad put them in a shoebox and set them on the low-overhanging shingled roof at the end of the house, near the outdoor stairs that led to the cookout area. I have no idea why he didn't bury them in the ground. He might have been in his Native American obsessive phase and wanted to give the puppies a Choctaw burial on a scaffold. Perhaps he wrapped fancy little blankets and sacred beads around them as well. Every time I walked past that end of the house, I eyed the roof nervously. I couldn't see the box, but I knew it was there, full of dead puppies decaying under the sun. I don't really remember what happened to the mother dog. She just had too many babies, and there is no remedy for the body when it is too small and required to do more than it can manage.

Years later, when I had my first child at the age of twenty-four, I lived in similar mountainous terrain in a rambling house in Malibu Canyon. One morning I looked across the room at my seven-month-old baby crawling across the den, and then I spotted the scorpion she was pulling herself toward, thinking it was some kind of strange toy. It was at that moment, I think, that I began to become a New Yorker. I wanted nothing more to do with desert arachnids, venomous snakes, or brush so dry it would ignite just from the sun.

Our home in Casitas Springs was a large ranch-style adobe and shingled house with a small backyard and a huge asphalt driveway and turnaround where I spent many hours riding my bike. The home site stood on the side of a brush- and cactus-covered mountain, about halfway to the top, and overlooked the dismal lower-middle-class community a quarter mile below. My father had bought the land, cut into the side of the mountain to create a level area on which to have his rough castle built, deposited me, my mother, and my three sisters there, and then went on the road for a decade.

Every couple of weeks someone—the previously mentioned folk singers, as well as addicts, preachers, or the occasional sex kitten— would drive up the long road to the house, usually late at night, usually drunk, looking for Johnny Cash. "He's not here!" my mother would shout, slamming the door on them.

We liked driving people away. We had a series of live-in housekeepers, one of whom quit the second day on the job because dinner had to be served at nine p.m. the night before due to unexpected guests. She left a note on the door to her room, a small apartment with a separate entrance attached to the house, explaining that she simply could not live with such erratic schedules and late mealtimes. It was probably the only time in my childhood that dinner had been delayed until that hour, but no matter. Good riddance to those who might intuit the strangeness. The only people I genuinely welcomed were those who performed services for us and then left— the carpet cleaner, the milkman, the Helms Bakery man, the gardener, and the Jewel-T delivery man, who brought a combination of snacks and household products. My mother had everything delivered, a practice I have since refined immeasurably as a New Yorker.

At five foot four and ninety-eight pounds, my mother was a small, nervous slip of a woman who lived on Winston cigarettes and coffee. She was deeply distracted by worry and rage about my father, who was not only constantly traveling, but also unfaithful and at the time using massive amounts of amphetamines and barbiturates. She eventually became so fragile and distant from us children, from her pain over her failing marriage, that I, as the oldest daughter, began to assume more of an adult role in the family. I was the fourth player at cards when couples came to visit her. I was the one my sisters turned to in times of trouble. I was the one who had to pretend not to be a child. I began to hate the very word "child," which seemed almost shameful—I remember how awkward it felt in my mouth and the unease it provoked to say it or hear it spoken. As if my mind could not reconcile with my age and my body, I began to have dreams that seemed frighteningly prescient, and visions that disturbed me.

I would often go into my parents' bedroom to look at my mother's clothes. She had a cocktail dress with a gold lamé bodice and a beige chiffon skirt, which I coveted with all my heart. I would open the long, mirrored sliding door to her closet and gaze at that dress until I'd memorized every detail of its appearance and texture. *This is what real women wear,* I thought, and I knew, as I fingered it longingly, that I would never own such a dress, because I would never be a real woman like my mother—because I would never smoke cigarettes or drink coffee, both of which repulsed me, and I was going to be five foot five and a half, and well over ninety-eight pounds: bigger than she, which was in poor taste and therefore unwomanly. I realized with absolute and sudden clarity one day while fondling the cocktail dress that if my life was going to be like this—not only being the fake girl, but now also being the fake adult when I was only eleven years old—that I did not wish to wear ankle socks anymore. The least everyone could do was to give me a pair of proper stockings and a garter belt. If I couldn't have the dress, I could at least have the undergarments that went with it.

I never cried, a fact in which I took great pride. But if nothing could reduce me to tears, everything had the potential to reduce me. My shoes and the feet inside of them reduced me to a paralysis of confidence. A broken zipper reduced me to eating baby cereal furtively, sitting alone in front of cartoons, at the ages of ten and eleven. Dead puppies reduced my future to a pinpoint. A scythe, which I swung wildly but to absolutely no effect at the waist-high weeds up by the cookout area near the built-in picnic table, reduced my forearm by a centimeter of skin, the scar of which I bear to this day.

My mother insisted on certain nightly rituals, which were as un-yielding as gravity. I had to curl my hair on pink foam rollers and I had to polish my shoes, a task I carried out with a numb, unfocused displeasure that grew into an acrid background fog that permeated my entire life. I had, as it happened, a problem with my feet. They were too big, bigger than my mother's—size 8½ to her delicate size 7 by the time I was twelve—and I was constantly injuring them. They were stung by bees and swelled up like balloons; they were smashed under overturned piano stools; they were cut by open sardine cans at the park; they demolished tiny things that came into their path. Everything about them was further evidence of my not being a real girl. My mother did not help matters by pointing out their defects, which I interpreted as meaning that no one would ever marry me. She also did not help by insisting that I wear oxfords—part of the school uniform—that were all white, rather than the much cooler black and white, which most of the other girls had. The whiteness of the shoes only accentuated the great length of my feet.

The other problem was my body, which in retrospect I think of as an adorable butterball but which at the time seemed like a corpu-lent rebuke to my mother. I famously broke the zipper on my moth-er's wedding gown when I tried it on at the age of ten, a story she took great pleasure in repeating for many years. She was very proud of her own ninety-eight pounds. Almost four decades later, I took her to meet her surgeon two weeks after she was diagnosed with lung cancer and two weeks before she died, following the surgery. She sat in the examining room on the white-papered table and lis-tened as he carefully described the surgical procedure he would perform on her. At the end of his speech, she said, nervously and only half joking, "And can you do something about this fat while you're in there?" By then she weighed about 140 pounds and was still perfectly beautiful.

When I was twelve, my parents finally split. My father was by then involved with June Carter, and my mother was with Dick Distin. Shortly after the divorce became final, they each married their new partners. My father was by now living in Tennessee, and my mother, Dick, and my sisters and I moved to Ventura, to another house on the hill overlooking the ocean. That house was a sixties fantasy come to life—a low-slung, single-story ranch with natural stone and rock accents. It had a tiny outdoor area and an enormous indoor pool area with hot pink furniture and awnings. A beaded curtain separated the sunken living room from the rest of the house. The den featured a wall made of boulders with a built-in oven, and my mother and Dick had a round bed in the master bedroom. My mother let me meet with an interior designer to select the colors and fabrics for my own bedroom, which had a sliding glass door leading to the pool area. I chose a lime green and royal blue palette, with a large floral print for the curtains and bedspread. The house was written up in the style section of the *Ventura Star–Free Press*, with several photos—including one of me in a bikini sitting by our indoor pool with the pink trimmings, looking, perhaps, a bit too self-consciously bemused.

It was as if, with that move, someone had opened all the windows and let the light and air inside. My mother almost immediately flourished, making a lot of friends, joining a garden club and a bowling league, taking dance lessons, playing card games, and hosting memorable parties. She crocheted, painted, gardened, renovated, organized, and collected. She became deeply involved in her church, and became close to many priests and nuns. She was vibrant. Because all my own friends loved her, a sizable group of teenagers inevitably gathered at our house. My mother remained in touch with two of my closest friends from high school until her death. They called her Viv. My dad had gotten clean and sober, and had bought an enormous, rough-hewn house of wood and stone perched on a bank of Old Hickory Lake in Hendersonville, twenty miles north of Nashville. Beginning when I was twelve, the summer after the divorce, my sisters and I began spending six weeks of the summer with him in Tennessee, as well as two weeks at Christmas break and the odd weekend when he would pick us up to take us on the road. He was physically a wreck that first summer, gaunt and hollow eyed, but by the next one he was whole and healthy and gaining weight.

Those summers of my early teens were glorious. Dad taught all of us to water-ski, and we swam in his giant rock pool that fed into the lake, and we went on long jeep rides at his farm in Bon Aqua, seventy miles from the lake house. We picked wild blackberries and he played guitar and we sang in the evenings. Out on the lawn after the sun went down, he made homemade peach ice cream with peaches from his orchard, setting off firecrackers while he cranked the ice cream maker. He cranked that old silver tub for an hour or more, but he never complained. He picked up all the kids in the extended family—June's sisters Helen's and Anita's kids, and various other children in the neighborhood—and took us to the movies when it was too hot to play outside. Sometimes he took us to three movies in a day. He rented the roller skating rink so we could skate together, undisturbed by fans.

By the summer of 1968, when I was thirteen, June and her two daughters, Carlene and Rosey, had moved in; June and my dad had married that March. One day I heard Carlene refer to my dad as "father." My hackles went up. She had her own father. He was *my* father. I said, "When did you start calling him that?" and I made it clear I didn't like it. She demurred and never called him father again.

By my mid-teens I was having summer flirtations with the sons of the accountants and musicians. I was going to dance clubs and swim parties and sometimes sitting in on Carlene's classes at Hendersonville High School when she started there in August, before I went back to California. I thought the kids my age in Tennessee were rubes, in general. I considered myself musically and stylistically sophisticated, refined by Woodstock-era and Southern California sensibilities, while they all seemed to be about a decade behind—I didn't know if they had even heard of Woodstock. I looked different, too. I was wearing bell-bottoms and had long, straight hair while most of the girls there were still in curls and skirts. Carlene, though, had a wild streak that didn't jibe with her Southern façade. The summer we were fourteen, she borrowed Bob Wootton's Harley-Davidson motorcycle, and I got on the back and we rode around the lake. The bike was so heavy that two small fourteen-year-old girls couldn't hold it up, so we just kept moving. We didn't stop anywhere, including intersections. My dad never knew we had taken the bike. He would have killed Bob.

Dad didn't tour when it was our summer vacation time with him. I didn't realize until much later how lucrative the summer touring was that he gave up to teach us to water-ski and make ice cream. He had signed a statement of promise when he married my mother saying that he would cooperate in raising their children as Catholics, and my mother was absolutely unwavering about this. He dutifully took us to Mass on Sundays and sat with us in the church, silent, never judging, never saying a word. When I was about fifteen, I finally told him I had no interest in going to Mass and I begged him not to make me go anymore. He looked at me with some surprise. I said I wouldn't tell my mother. I could see this caused him a moral dilemma, but by the time I was sixteen, he'd relented. I didn't have to go to Mass anymore. He said that at sixteen I was old enough to make my own decision. He continued to take my sisters for a while longer. I felt a little guilty about not going to church at all, having never missed Mass for my entire life, so I experimented with Southern Baptist and Evangelical religion for a short time, thinking I would try exactly what my mother most judged and feared, and something closer to my dad's heart and upbringing, but that didn't turn out well for me. I didn't like the lack of dignity and personal boundaries in the free-for-all shouting and preaching and laying on of hands, and I realized I enjoyed the rituals of religion far more than the substance. I was more Catholic by nature than I had known.

Interestingly, my dad didn't go in for the overt emotionalism of his own religion, either. He had powerful religious beliefs, but he seldom went to church.

When I was sixteen, he took Kathy and Rosey and me to Europe with him, my first trip abroad. We visited Anne Frank's house in Amsterdam, which made an indelible imprint. I found I was more a natural traveler than anything else, and that trip began a lifelong series of sojourns to Europe, and more generally a life circumscribed by travel.

It was during this period that a great, gray fog seemed to lift from my family for a few years. My dad was at a peak of success and health. He was gaining in physical and artistic power, and his television show was a huge hit. After Bob Dylan or Joni Mitchell or any of the icons of my youth were guests on his show, I went to school the next day bursting with confidence and pride. I basked in that reflected glory. Both of my parents were flush with romance and exuberance in their new marriages, and I was feeling the first stirrings of my own independence. I went to high school at St. Bonaventure in Ventura and wore my Catholic uniform skirt very short. I had my first boyfriend, and I fell in with a small group of classmates who were a little left of center, like me. We called ourselves the "Anarchy Society." The Anarchists managed to wield enough power and votes to elect me senior princess for homecoming, to great consternation and protest from the "rah-rahs." My dad got me tickets to see the Rolling Stones in Los Angeles and he bought me a car. I briefly fell in with a surfer crowd, although I never fit in with them. I began to nurture magnificent surges of melancholy and longing, which I attempted to turn into bad poetry. I finally began to break loose from the internal pressure of religious and domestic constriction, and to understand what I loved and who I might become.

If Magritte had painted my childhood, it would be a chaos of floating snakes, white oxfords, dead Chihuahuas, and pink hair rollers. Bolts of gold lamé and chiffon would be draped over everything, stained with coffee and burned with cigarettes, and garden hoes would be wielded by drunks with guitars. Glass jars full of spiders and amphetamines would line the walls behind the sliding mirrored doors. The landscape would be barren and steep and full of animal treachery. There is nothing green. There is no oxygen. I am a foreigner in this painting. I look at it as if in a museum. I can talk about the color of the oils and the depth of field, how the two dimensions feel like three when I know there are four, but I cannot be a line drawing or even an abstract smudge in the center and survive to describe it.

Sometimes, in my present life, when I am lying awake in the night with the Nameless Dread, if I can trace it back to the school on the hill, the house on the hill, the car lights wandering up the long drive to park at our door and ring our bell, to the sound of pouring coffee, the smell of cigarettes, the rattlesnakes who lived just beyond the fence, the dead Chihuahuas in the shoebox on the roof, the tarantulas and scorpions in mayonnaise jars, the scythe and the waist-high weeds which I whacked so hard that I swung around and whacked myself in the forearm, if I can conjure these pictures to attach to the dread, then I can free myself from the present moment and I sleep. But most of the time I avoid such conjuring. Most of the time I don't go back at all. Most of the time I stand next to Magritte.

Of the many delivery vehicles that made their way up the steep hill to our Casitas Springs home, the Helms Bakery truck was my favorite, and I would always run outside when I heard it bump across the cattle grate at the top of the drive. One day I bolted out through the garage to greet the driver just as he flung open the back doors as if he were revealing the mysteries of a gypsy wagon. I practically swooned at the sight of hundreds of cakes, pies, tarts, and breads.

"Do you take the truck home at night?" I asked.

"Yes." He smiled at me.

"How do you keep from eating all this stuff when you get home?"

"Well, if you're around it all day, you want to get away from it when you go home at night. Does your daddy sit around and sing all day when he comes home off the road?"

I pondered for a moment. "Well, no."

It was the answer he expected, and so I gave it, but what I was thinking then, and what I understand more clearly now, is that it's not just the singing you bring home with you. It's the constant measuring of ideas and words if you are a songwriter, and the daily handling of your instrument if you are a musician, and the humming and scratching and pushing and testing of the voice, the reveling in the melodies if you are a singer. More than that, it is the effort to straddle two worlds, and the struggle to make the transition from the creative realms to those of daily life and back with grace. My father did all of those, as a habit of being. He provided a template for me, of how to live with integrity as an artist day to day.

I belong to an extended family of musicians whose members sprawl across generations. Some occupy positions of great acclaim (my father and my stepmother's family, the Carters), some have modest but respectable careers marked by persistence and hard work (my uncle Tommy Cash), while others never made it much further than anecdotal obscurity (my maternal uncle "Wildman" Ray Liberto, a onetime raucous honky-tonk piano player with a handlebar mustache), and some are just embarking (my daughter Chelsea). At sixteen I did not intend to take my place among them. Tradition was anathema to me; I understood that any real rebellion in which I could engage would involve taking a nondomestic, or artistic but nonmusical, path. My mother had had a strict Italian Catholic upbringing, which pretty much defined her views about a woman's place in the world, and my father was an enormously visible performer. I had a fierce though silent desire to live a different life. I would not be a housewife, nor would I seek fame as a singer. I would be an archaeologist and move to a kibbutz. (An odd choice for a Catholic girl, perhaps, but so much the better.) I would go to medical school and write poetry. Change and newness: They would define my life.

Then, when I was a day out of high school, my father took me on the road. It was something of a graduation gift, and a chance to catch up on some of the time we had lost. Traveling the world, watching him perform, and singing on the bus were also the basis for a serious education. Early on he made a list of a hundred essential country songs, which he instructed me to learn, a wide-ranging selection that ran from old history-lesson songs like "The Battle of New Orleans" to classics like Hank Williams's "I'm So Lonesome I Could Cry." As I was ushered into this treasury of song, it was thrilling to learn more about my father through his great love for the music. I learned to play guitar from my stepmother's sister Helen, from Mother Maybelle Carter, and from Carl Perkins, all of whom were on the road with Dad at the time. Each day I spent many hours in dressing rooms, practicing chords and the old songs they taught me. I discovered a passion for songwriting that remains undiminished to this day and that led me into my life as a writer and singer—into my family's vocation.

At the heart of all real country music lies family, lies a devotion to exploring the bonds of blood ties, both in performance and in songwriting. Of course, there have been notable families in pop music—the Jacksons, the Beach Boys, the Everly Brothers—and parents and children have sung all manner of music together or in succession—Judy Garland and Liza Minnelli, Nat King Cole and Natalie Cole, Tim Buckley and Jeff Buckley, Hank Williams and his progeny, Loudon Wainwright III and his children. But the community of country music has always emphasized the family connection, reveling in it, and there seems to be both less rivalry among its members and less need for its children to break away on their own musical terms. (Although that was an impulse that I struggled with mightily for the first fifteen years of my own career.) Country and roots music treat family as a rich and fascinating source of material for its songs.

As a teenager, I saw the Earl Scruggs Revue perform perhaps twenty times and held my breath for those moments when laconic Earl would glance at one of his sons, who had just performed a phenomenal solo, in a fleeting moment of approbation. Doc and Merle Watson also had a special resonance for me as performers in that they were so close—in their genetic gifts, in their attitudes, and in their quiet respect for each other—that it was a privilege to be in their audience. I was certain that they treated each other the same offstage as on. When Merle died in 1985, it was painful to imagine the enormity of the loss for Doc. He lost not only his son but his musical soul mate. It is comforting to know that Doc now plays music with his grandson, Merle's son.

It was riveting in a different respect to watch the Judds at the height of their career work out their mother-daughter tensions onstage. Every subtle gesture—Naomi stroking Wynonna's hair and the almost imperceptible flinch it provoked, or the intense glances from one to the other that were ignored—spoke volumes, and every adult daughter in the audience could relate. In my own performing, I've found it impossible to stay mad at anyone I love when I'm onstage with him or her. Arguments and grudges melt away under the spotlights and the audience's gaze. I feel that I should somehow be better onstage, more magnanimous, and sometimes I *am* better. One of the sweetest moments of my life occurred the last time my dad played Carnegie Hall. I had been a little angry with him the day before the show and had brought up some old grievances, which he listened to with patient grace. After hearing me out, he invited me to sing "I Still Miss Someone" with him the next night. I demurred. The day of the performance, he asked me if I had changed my mind and would join him onstage. I had a fierce headache and told him again that I could not do it. I went to his hotel that evening before the performance, and for the third time, he asked me to join him during the show. I declined once more, but as I watched him walk out of the room, there was something about the look of his back, and the look of him walking away, and the memory of the thousands of times I had seen his strong back from the wings as he faced an audience, that made me suddenly realize what it meant to him. I called after him. "Dad. I'll do it," I said. That night, as we sang together, all the old pain dissolved. I felt the longing to connect completely satisfied. Under the lights, in the safety of a few thousand people who loved us like crazy just then, I got something from my dad that I'd been trying to get since I was about six years old. Oddly, I don't think we'd ever been as close.

Performed by families and often about family, traditional country music spares nothing and no one in its gaze. In the deeply morbid early country songs about topics like dead babies, for example, lie the hard truths about mountain life. The best in this tragic genre—according to my dad, anyway—is an old tune called "The Engineer's Dying Child." The engineer's baby is sick, but he has to go to work and drive ol' No. 9, or whatever number it is, and so bids his wife:

*Just hang a light when I pass tonight—*
*Hang it so it can be seen.*
*If the baby's dead, then show the red;*
*If it's better, then show the green.*

Happily the engineer sees green, but most infants did not fare so well in early Appalachian songs, which provided a way to take account of the losses and gather comfort.

A mother is the most revered member of the family in traditional country music, a figure whose mention holds the greatest emotional charge. The "country classic of them all" (again, according to Dad) is "Sweeter Than the Flowers," cowritten by Ervin Rouse, who also wrote "Orange Blossom Special." It begins:

*Yes, as far as I can remember*
*She'll remain the rose of my heart.*
*Mom took sick along in December;*
*February brought us broken hearts.*
*The reason we've not called a fam'ly reunion,*
*We knew that she wouldn't be there,*
*But since we've thought it all over, Mama,*
*We know that your spirit is there.*

If this is not wrenching enough, the song continues (with a line that boasts one of the all-time great rhymes):

*No, no, there's no need to bother;*
*To speak of you now would only hurt father.*

This couplet just kills me, so to speak.

Modern country music speaks less of such desperate loss, and has become shiny and rich and rather shallow as a result. The dead have all but disappeared, though they do occasionally surface. Back in the eighties, George Jones's "He Stopped Loving Her Today" had everyone swooning with morbid joy.

The family has likewise faded in country, as sexual heat has begun to obsess most singers and songwriters, just as it does in pop music. Anyone who has listened to old honky-tonk knows that pairing up and breaking up has always been a theme of country, but today it is *the* theme: The airwaves are soggy with songs about romance, desire, longing for love, love that got away, love gone wrong, standing up to or by your man or woman, loneliness, frustration, carnal passion, lovers' quarrels, and on and on. It's all legitimate subject matter, certainly, and good fodder for song, but the hormonal flushes of love affairs are not the only thing going on in a life. Mostly hidden from view are the other potent relationships, forged of blood and shared history, rich with emotional content, ripe for exploration. As Bruce Springsteen—one of the most family-inspired songwriters of the last two decades—said in "Highway Patrolman," "Nothing feels better than blood on blood."

．　．　．　．　．

I lasted for two and a half years on the bus with my father until, feeling the constraint a young girl feels in the constant presence of a parent, I moved to London. But an important part of my heart and soul was given form and expression on that bus, and I came to realize how a shared passion forges deep bonds between people, defining a family more deeply than blood connection alone could do. Years later I called my dad to ask him about the old songs—particularly songs about mothers, babies, brothers and sisters, fathers and grandparents. He gave me titles, years, and the names of the recording artists, and then sang them to me over the phone, verse by verse, growing more excited with each new recollection. As he had an appointment to keep, he told me to call back the following day so we could continue to talk about the songs "for a long time."

"I know *all* of them!" he boasted happily.

I thought about those old songs all night long and called him back first thing the next morning so he could sing the entirety of "Sweeter Than the Flowers" to me. He paused at the end as I scribbled down the lyrics.

"There's a whole other group of songs, if you're interested," he said.

"About what?" I asked.

"Dead dogs," he answered solemnly, and proceeded to rattle off a list of titles.

I laughed, but what I was really thinking about was that bakery truck back in Casitas Springs and how I had lied to the driver. We do take our deliveries home at night, and everything comes inside, and we're not shy about getting our fill.

There have been very few times when I could say with certainty that my life would change irrevocably in the course of a day. In fact, there may have been only this one occasion. I am more accustomed to lethargy and emotional sputtering when working up to a life transition, but January 5, 1976, was different. I was twenty years old. At around midnight I was sitting on a beach near Montego Bay. I had been in Jamaica for about a month with my dad and stepmother at their house, Cinnamon Hill, an eighteenth-century sugar plantation great house, originally built and owned for over two hundred years by the family of the poet Elizabeth Barrett Browning. (She never visited Cinnamon Hill herself, due to fragile health, but many of her ancestors and their descendants are buried just down the hill from the house in the Barrett family cemetery.)

In the three years before that January night, I had spent many weeks at Cinnamon Hill. Though the house was haunted—a fact freely acknowledged by skeptics and believers alike—and creaky and a bit damp, I loved it beyond reason. Its battered stone walls, two feet thick in some places, had withstood a hundred hurricanes. Massive mahogany beams crossed the fourteen-foot ceilings of the drawing room, and its floors were of the same wood, polished to a high cherry gloss. Growing on the property were wild orchids, palms, bougainvillea, and every variety of fern and Caribbean broad-leafed plant, and from checkerboard-tiled porches on three sides of the house one could enjoy the aromatic breezes and middle-distance view of the ocean. In the front yard, near the palm-lined white stone drive, were two cannons from the old town of Port Royal, which had sunk completely into the sea after an earthquake in the seventeenth century, and an enormous corroded lead basin that had been used to stir the boiling sugar in Cinnamon Hill's eighteenth-century heyday. (On a trip to Jamaica many years later, Bill Murray, who was filming a comedy special with his brothers on the Cinnamon Hill golf course, came by for a visit. When he saw the giant basin in the yard, now overflowing with vines and blossoms, he remarked, "I love what you've done with your wok.")

The whole estate was resonant with the lives and deaths of Barretts, the history of the Jamaican sugarcane industry, and the rich and languid temper of island life.

We had massive bonfires on the beach over Christmas and New Year's holidays with our close friends the Rollinses, candlelit dinners with the shutters thrown wide open on the deep-set windows, and a Southern black-eyed pea lunch at the Rollinses' on New Year's Day, where every pea consumed represented a dollar to be made in the coming year.

My father and John Rollins, two very large and charismatic men, presided over all the holiday events with tremendous humor, generosity, intelligence, and largeness of spirit. Although they were best friends, my father tended to defer to John Rollins in subtle ways in conversation, due to John's greater age and vaster wealth and his ability to genially command the world around him to bend to his ideas and plans. I cannot think of another person, apart from his own father, to whom my father responded in that particular way. I adored John Rollins, who was a superb raconteur with a refined sense of irony, and truly a self-made man. As a boy, he had studied obituaries in the newspaper to find when a funeral was taking place so he could unobtrusively slip into the family wake and get a free meal. Although by 1976 he was one of the richest men in the country, he and my father would try to "out-poor" each other at the dinner table with stories of their childhoods of abject poverty.

Now the holiday festivities were over, and I was at the precipice of a new life. I had been on the road with my dad for two and a half years, I had managed to get in a year's college credits, and I was restless. I was moving to London the very next day and I had gone down to the beach to ritualize this event, if only to myself. I was nursing a broken heart, and I wanted to put the Atlantic Ocean between myself and Randy Scruggs. This was not the only reason I was moving to England, but it was a good enough one at the time. Randy and I had never had a relationship, beyond a few awkward dates where he sat in my dad's living room and played his guitar while I listened rapturously. But I had a longing, both for him and even more for the idea of him. I had been nurturing a fantasy of joining our two families, musically and personally, and I was riveted by Randy's quiet but intense demeanor, both in person and onstage. I went to see him play with his dad and brothers in the Earl Scruggs Revue so many times—just about every place they played in the South. I had held out hope for a year or so that Randy was my destiny, but I had recently learned that he was going to marry. The thought of London had been in the back of my mind for years, and this seemed like the perfect time to go.

Jeff and Ted Rollins, John's sons, a few years younger than I, had followed me down to the beach. They tended to follow me around a lot in Jamaica. The boys sat very quietly on the sand as I stared at the sky and listened to the waves. More than an hour went by in this reverie, with the boys just waiting for me, never saying a word. I cannot remember the specifics of any epiphanies, only that I was overcome with a vague but grand sense of limitless possibility for my life, and an almost painful feeling of excitement and happiness. It seems impossible now to think of being so full of feelings that were utterly unambiguous. I don't believe I have felt so strong a rush of unadulterated optimism and joy since that night. I was happy without the slightest tinge of poignancy, or underlying anxiety, about how my plans for the future might affect anyone else. Anything could happen to me, and whatever it might be could only be magnificent.

I was about to go through immigration at the Montego Bay airport the following day when I realized that I had left my coat at Cinnamon Hill. I was going to step off the plane in London into a winter day, and I was wearing only a girlish, almost infantile sundress of pale blue, with short puff sleeves and a modest square neck, that came just to my knees. Ted Rollins, ever present and so eager to please, immediately volunteered to have Dad's security guard drive him at top speed to Cinnamon Hill to retrieve the coat. He brought it to me minutes before my flight took off, and I hurled thank-yous at him as I sprinted happily out onto the tarmac. I took my seat in first class—Dad treated me very well in those years I spent with him after high school—next to a distinguished-looking English gentleman. After quizzically looking me up and down, he leaned over and said with a smile, "Pardon me, but could you sign this paper for my daughter? I'm sure you are a very famous rock star, and I don't know who you are, but she will know."

Embarrassed, I said, "No, sir, I'm not. She wouldn't know who I am."

He shoved the paper at me. "Please," he said, and smiled again. I signed the paper, flushed, guilty, and excited. My new life was in full swing, and the plane hadn't even taken off.

I arrived in London with the sheen of anticipatory greatness worn a bit dull due to exhaustion and creeping uncertainty. From the view in Jamaica, London was nothing less than Oz. Emerging from customs, it was just a big, crowded airport. Hundreds of people, looking for other travelers, fixed their eyes on me momentarily as I came through the automatic doors into the terminal. I was alarmed and started to turn around. A throng of tired new arrivals were at my heels, and I swung back around and pushed my cart forward, red faced and grim.

In 1976 I was, despite my grand plans and bravado, a timid girl. I had asked a member of the sound crew from my father's last European tour with whom I had become friendly to meet me at the airport and drop me at my hotel. I passed the crowd and the length of the barricade without seeing him. I waited near the front doors to the terminal until he showed up, nearly half an hour later. He seemed distracted and not terribly happy to see me and quickly ushered me into his car, where we rode in silence to my hotel. When I mentioned getting together later, he mumbled that he had plans. It was the only time I saw him during the six months I lived in England.

I had sent my trunk ahead of me, which had been retrieved by the copresidents of my father's fan club in Britain, a kind and devoted couple who were very gracious and solicitous of my welfare as a young girl on my own in a foreign country. They had shown up at the airport unannounced just as my other ride arrived, but I was eager to go off with the young man, who held the promise of excitement and fun and new friends, and I politely declined their offer of a ride. They invited me to their house for dinner several times over the next few months, but I had decided that they were probably dull and conservative and imagined strained conversations about my father over glasses of sherry. I always found an excuse not to go. To this day I feel twinges of guilt about my lack of appreciation and courtesy.

I stayed at the Portman Hotel for three weeks while I looked for an apartment. Dreary Portman Square was full of sullen businessmen passing through in gray suits, but it was the only hotel I knew, as I had stayed there on my last trip to London, and I did not have imagination enough to search out a better place.

My dad had arranged a job for me at his label, CBS Records. I had begun a major in music theory at the community college I'd attended, but I had no real understanding of how the music business worked and no office skills whatsoever.

Maurice Oberstein, the president of the UK division of the label, met with me in his office and asked about my interests and abilities, graciously treating me as if I were a valuable new asset to the company rather than a favor to be done for the child of one of his top artists.

I was nervous and subdued, but I gamely tried to present myself as a young woman who would bring a fresh perspective to the company. At the end of the conversation, Obie told me that he would pay me forty pounds a week, under the table, and assigned me to the position of assistant in the artist relations department under the supervision of Derek Witt, über-publicist and the first outright queen I ever knew. Derek's codirector in the artist relations department was Anthea Joseph, legendary cofounder of the Troubadour in London. When Bob Dylan arrived in London in 1963, he brought a note with him from Pete Seeger: "Find the Troubadour. Ask for Anthea." She was the first person to put him on a London stage, and she is immortalized in one scene of the epic 1967 Dylan documentary *Don't Look Back*, in which she is being reassured by Bob after a hotel glass-breaking incident. Her main job at CBS seemed to be smoking heavily and having lengthy and intense phone conversations and lunches with musicians, artists, Communists, and intellectuals of all sorts.

Anthea had a tremendous influence on me. Her intellectual

rigor, combined with an eccentric personality and a passion for music, was absolutely riveting—as was her own oddness. Tall and angular, with a great gap between her two front teeth, stringy brown hair, and social service wire-rimmed glasses, she wore narrow jeans and low-heeled boots as a virtual uniform, which in 1976 I read as sartorial code for an anarchist. It was thrilling. Her perpetual expression was one of bemusement at some private joke combined with an intense, piercing gaze. At the same time she had a permanent air of exasperation because she knew no one could ever meet her intensity head-on. She was the subject of an inordinate amount of gossip and resentment from people in the department who complained that she didn't actually do any work, but I thought we were incredibly lucky that she deigned to show up at all. I longed to know what Anthea knew. I wanted to listen in on her conversations, and I wanted her experience and her biting tongue. My own intellectual rigor was nonexistent and my sophistication was nascent at best, but Anthea was extraordinarily tolerant of me, even congenial, and I knew her feelings were genuine, because she never hesitated to take me to task when she felt it was warranted.

I developed a friendship, and a terrible crush, on Malcolm Eade, a young man whose office was at the opposite end of the floor from mine on the way to the coffee room. I managed to make myself available to fetch coffee for everyone in the department, several times a day, so that I could stop by Malcolm's office for a chat, or just peer in at him soulfully as I went by. He was fair-haired and boyish, well mannered and shy, which at the time seemed to me to be a great deal to recommend any man my age. I spent so much time in his office that it's hard to believe I didn't get him fired. I myself could not be fired, as I did not have a real job, but Malcolm, in his kindness, allowed me to test the parameters of my newly formed and awkward notions of enticement as I sat in the chair opposite his desk. Nothing ever happened between us, not even a kiss, but I had never felt so perfectly accepted by any man. I tried out all sorts of personalities and opinions in front of Malcolm, and if I tested his patience, he never once let on. If Anthea was a slightly terrifying but endlessly compelling role model, Malcolm was a seductive and innocent dream.

I was given a desk that was crammed into the corner of the office of a department staff member, David, and it somehow never managed to cross my mind that he might well have considered me an intruder: Johnny Cash's kid on a lark in London, taking up a good deal of his space for the purpose of absolutely nothing that he could ascertain. Still, he was kind, and did not even resent his orders from Derek to take me around to find a flat. David did suggest that we tell prospective landlords that I was his secretary, "to make things smoother." I self-importantly balked at this, as he was not senior enough to have a secretary, and the plan felt strangely lascivious to me, but I see now that that little ego stroke was the very least I could give him in return. Eventually, he did help me locate a flat, a small, lovely third-floor walk-up at No. 3 Carlingford Road, in Hampstead. (Later, I met David's fiancée, an immaculately put-together and aggressive blonde who favored shiny suits in shades of steel gray with matching stiletto-heeled boots, had perfectly straight and sleek almost-white hair, and wore near–Kabuki-style makeup. She scared me to death, though she dripped honey when she spoke. One evening shortly after my arrival, as we were having drinks after work at a wine bar, she thoroughly looked me over and said thoughtfully, and not unkindly, "You aren't very glamorous, are you?" I didn't answer, in part because I wasn't sure if I should be insulted, and in part because I wasn't sure what the answer was. After many years of wrestling with that question, I decided that she was partly correct. I like a little glamour, just not so obvious, and a bit more rock and roll than business dominatrix.

It soon became clear that my job in artist relations would involve little more than deciding which seats various people in the company would be given for concerts by CBS artists performing in London, and then doling out the tickets when they came to David's and my office to retrieve them. At one point, when several artists were playing in London at the same time, David and I posted a sign on our door that read CBS BOX OFFICE. QUEUE HERE. (By the end of my London stay, a few Anglicisms had seeded themselves into my mind, forever to remain: the proper use and spelling of the word "queue," the reversal of month and day when writing a date, and an obsessive and unrelenting adherence to teatime, with proper tea brewed in a pot.) When we strategized seat placements for concerts, we began with the given that Obie always got center orchestra, six to eight rows back from the stage, depending on the venue. After Obie and his wife, there was a strict hierarchy for bestowing seats, with the heads of each department at the top and with secretaries at the very bottom. This pecking order was taken with utmost seriousness, and it was an unspeakable breach of protocol to give a mediocre seat to a self-inflated A&R guy. When I inadvertently made such assignments in my early days at the job, I would get a personal visit from the offended party, which would leave me withered, shaking, and in tears. I felt sorry for the secretaries, who were mostly relegated to the balconies, and even sorrier for the occasional member of the cleaning staff who ventured to ask for a ticket to see a favorite artist, to whom I was ordered to give back-of-the-balcony seats. I sometimes managed to elude David's observant eye to give one of these lower-echelon workers a center orchestra seat.

The CBS office building was in Soho Square, just off Oxford Street. I took the tube to work every morning from Hampstead and got off at the Tottenham Court Road station. My office was on the sixth floor, and I strove, with utmost diligence and gut-churning dread, to stay away from The Third Floor, which housed A&R and promotion. No woman was safe there; the taunts and come-ons were urgent, and not friendly. The men in those two departments were notorious: loud, predatory, debauched, and dependably drunk by four in the afternoon. They started drinking, as well as ingesting other substances, early in the afternoon, and most of the women I knew in the company absolutely refused to go to the third floor anytime after lunch. In the mornings, when they were still hungover, it was relatively safe if you got in and out quickly; if it was essential to go there in the afternoon, you took a friend. Whenever I had to deliver tickets or a memo there, I would step out of the elevator and stand frozen in terror for several minutes, sweating and trying to calm myself, nearly coming out of my skin in fear, before I could work up the courage to push open the double doors to their offices. Sometimes, going down in the elevator to the lobby, I could hear a muffled roar as we passed The Floor, and I would shudder in relief as I glided past in a silent, sealed box.

The staff of the art department was equally crazy but without the misogyny and maliciousness of the promotion guys, and I became friends with several of them. They teased me mercilessly about my American ignorance. I was told that corgis were the queen's favorite breakfast cereal, that the town Slough was pronounced "sloff," and that black pudding was made of cherries. I was the source of a tremendous amount of amusement for the lads who did up the album covers, and, actually, I was glad to oblige.

I loved Hampstead, and I loved the image of myself there, as a young and slightly starving albeit plump artist in formation, alone but comfortably taken care of in a nice flat in an expensive part of town, with the rent paid by my dad. I tried to live on the forty pounds a week, but it was not easy, given the proximity of the antique markets at the top of Hampstead High Street. I had developed a serious penchant for antiques at the age of eighteen, a love which has stayed with me throughout my life, and I spent most of my money on old teacups and plates and ivory-handled fish knives. Whenever I was at home in my flat, I began listening to four records on continuous rotation: Bob Dylan's *Desire*, Tammy Wynette and David Houston's album of duets, James Taylor's *Gorilla*, and Janis Ian's *Society's*

*Child.* These four records wore grooves in my personality, I listened to them so much. They held the entire content of my experience and my hopes. I had no interest in going to the Heath, the nearby park that everyone went on about as being so beautiful and peaceful. I did not care about peace and nature in the least; what I cared about was music, men, food, antiques, excitement, and being pretty.

I quickly became very close to a girl named Sandra Cooper, who was a couple of years younger than me and worked on the artist relations floor as a temp. Sandra had an identical twin sister, Brenda, who also occasionally worked on the same floor and who lived with one of the lighting directors for the band Yes. Although Sandy was initially suspicious of me and avoided me, I was attracted to her, mostly because she had a bracingly caustic attitude and a fierce, musical laugh. One day I passed her desk on the way to my crammed office and made a joke to her about having to go to the third floor, and she opened up immediately. She and Brenda were both very fashionable, very thin, perfectly made up, and always tottering on extremely high heels. I took their lead and bought a pair of six-inch wedged heels, which I wore constantly (except for days it snowed), and a brown velvet blazer. I also invested in a pair of Fiorucci jeans, very tight, to try to look more like them, but my size 32's did not have quite the same effect as their size 28's. Sandy and Brenda and I started going to lunch together every day, usually to a Greek restaurant near Soho Square that served grilled grapefruit as an appetizer followed by souvlaki or kebabs. As Sandy and

I were constantly broke, Brenda, who was nicely taken care of by her music business boyfriend and who had her own income from different sources, mostly relating to fashion, paid for our meals. Brenda wore a red baseball cap every day of her life due to a chronic displeasure with her hair. One day, a couple of months into our friendship, she showed up at lunch panicked, because she had to attend a black-tie event and could not figure out how to make the baseball cap go with her evening gown. I never saw the top of her head during my entire stay in England. I loved the twins' energy, their toughness, and their good-natured, and sometimes vicious, sniping at each other. They showed me how to thicken my own skin, how to dry up some of my cloying natural sentimentality and cultivate a more urbane sense of humor. I would never have had the courage to become the person I was turning into without both Anthea's template for intellectual and musical depth and the wild influence of the Cooper twins.

I was, I began to notice, gaining weight. The year before I had had a tumor removed from my left ovary, and had begun to develop another before I left for England. My doctor at home had started me on an injectable hormone that I had to receive every three months, which tended to make me fat. Soon after my arrival I found a private doctor in Belgravia who consented to administer the injections. The first time I visited him, I was led into his inner office, superbly appointed with mahogany and leather, and was shown to a seat in front of his polished desk. He smiled in greeting and said, "Well, first thing, let's see your figure." I had to stand and remove my brown velvet blazer, and turned slowly around in front of him in a state of increasing mortification. My figure was by this point dumpy and broad in the hips, and I could see by his curt nod that he thought so as well. He gave me the shot every couple of months, for an extraordinary fee, and I just continued to grow heavier.

Early in my stay in London, the second day of my friendship with Sandy, we went to the Hard Rock Cafe, which in 1976 was brand new and outrageously trendy. It was cold, so we walked quickly from the Portman, and every man who walked by us turned to stare frankly at Sandy. She suggested we join arms so that they would think we were lovers, and we linked together. The male stares now became embarrassed glances, and Sandy played the routine up, squeezing me and whispering in my ear. We entered the Hard Rock, and again all the male eyes in the place turned toward Sandy. As soon as we sat down, a young man came directly over to her and asked her to join him and his friends. She responded with a withering comment, which I can no longer recall, and he recoiled and walked away silently. The few seconds that passed between his invitation and her reply were torture for me. Not knowing the rules, I was terrified that she would leave me sitting alone at this very prominent table, swathed in brown velvet, with my lackluster haircut, swollen body, dearth of makeup, and Dubonnet on ice. I was inexpressibly grateful and loved her for her loyalty.

It was at the Hard Rock, on a subsequent visit with Sandy, maybe a week or two later, that I heard Bruce Springsteen for the first time. Everyone had been talking about him. I had read about him in *Melody Maker*, like everyone else in the music business in London, but I had not yet heard his music. I was sitting at the bar at the Hard

Rock, Dubonnet in hand, when "Born to Run" came on the sound system. Sandy was talking to me, but I could not hear a word she was saying, so riveted was I to the music. The combination of urgency, poetry, testosterone-fueled guitars, and the relentless backbeat made me literally weak in the knees. It was as if William Blake had put on black leather and climbed a motorcycle. I was enraptured. I couldn't begin to conceive that, thirty-three years later, I would do a duet with Bruce Springsteen on my album *The List*. That concept belonged to someone else's life in 1976, not the shy, round girl sitting at the bar of the Hard Rock Cafe in London.

I turned twenty-one while I was in London but thought it cool and grown-up not to let anyone know. For that weekend I arranged to go to Scotland with some of the people from CBS to stay at the huge manor house of one of our artists, a country singer who also worked the oil rigs in the North Sea. His wife, who was from the American South, made cornbread and black-eyed peas for dinner, dished out with a thick regional accent. Beginning to miss my mother, with whom I had not lived since the day after I graduated from high school, I decided to tell a few people it was my birthday, and they came up with a cake for me. I lay awake a long time in a small guest bedroom that night, thinking of my mother, my sisters, my father, and the fact that no one in my family was there to witness my turning into an adult.

I saw a lot of bands play in London, including a reunion concert of the Small Faces, which I went to alone. Some sort of reception was held after the show, which I attended mostly because a free buffet was promised. (Under normal circumstances, an evening meal was nonexistent for me unless someone took me out.) At around one a.m. I suddenly found myself in a near-deserted basement room with a pillaged buffet table and not a soul I knew anywhere around. I had counted on getting a ride home from David or Anthea, as I thought they would surely be at the show and the reception, or from someone else I knew who had a car or a bit of money, as I did not have a penny on me. I panicked for a moment, not knowing how I would get home, and I realized that I had no choice but to walk the few miles to Hampstead in the freezing early hours. I gathered my thoughts into a singular point. I banished my fear of being alone on the streets in the middle of the night. I did not allow any other possibility to enter my mind other than a long trudge and a safe arrival. I set out in my very high-heeled boots and marched myself up through Piccadilly, on through Camden Town and Mornington Crescent, up Hampstead Road and along to No. 3 Carlingford Road. It was bitterly cold, and I was tortured by my ill-advised footwear. My entire body screaming in protest, I kept my eyes forward and my anxiety under wraps, and arrived home at around four a.m., where I fell immediately into bed. That walk was the dividing line in my life, marking the boundary between my former unformed, raw, swollen personality and the more emotionally sinuous, urbane girl I became. There would be periods in my future when the old girl would take possession of me for a few weeks or months, but from then on I had the blueprint, devised on the long walk, and the determination, also inaugurated in those few hours, to escape from the inundation of her dark, turgid spirit.

·   ·   ·   ·   ·

In the early summer of 1976 I went home to Nashville for a brief visit. The first thing my dad announced after greeting me was, "That's enough. You need to stay home now. You need to move back to the United States." I was stunned. He did not say this in a pleading or coercive way, but simply delivered it as an edict. I did not even think to argue with him, his effect was so forceful, but I made a feeble remark about having to go back and pick up my belongings. He dismissed this instantly. He told me to have my girlfriends pack my trunk, and to deal with terminating my sublease by long distance. I called Brenda, who I had gradually grown closer to than Sandy over the past few months, and she and Sandy packed up my trunk with my clothes and records and antique dishes, and shipped it to Nashville. I called Derek and told him I wasn't coming back. I called the real estate agent and told him I was vacating the flat. I applied to Vanderbilt University for the coming September, found out I was lacking a math credit, and hired a private tutor to teach me trigonometry. I realized much later that Dad was afraid I would disappear from his life; that I would become a permanent expatriate and lose touch with my family and my roots. He told me years later that he had a fear that I would be lost to them forever if I stayed in Europe any longer. He was probably right.

Brenda came to see me in Nashville late that summer. As we sat by the pool at Dad's house on the lake, I was miserable, hating her for being so beautiful when I was bloated with hormones, hating her for having a return ticket to London. It had not even occurred to me— and it wouldn't occur to me for another twenty years—that I could have argued with my father and simply gone back. It seemed a bad moment for my old, limp personality to resurface, but in retrospect, I'm grateful he could see the possible trajectories of my life, and intervened to keep me connected to him and the rest of my family.

"We found your journal when we were packing your trunk," Brenda suddenly declared. "Sandy started to read it aloud, but I told her it was wrong, that we shouldn't read it and she should stop, because you were so lonely." She looked at me steadily. "You were *so* lonely," she said again, almost accusingly.

I hated her for knowing more about me than I knew about myself.

The next time I saw her, several years later, she and Sandy were both living in New York. I spent one wild weekend with them there, and they tried to set me up with a young man who told me confidentially that he was considering the priesthood. We went to a lot of clubs and parties and ended up at the Green Kitchen, in Hell's Kitchen, at five a.m. on a Monday. I crawled back to my tiny room at the Berkshire Hotel later that morning, deeply depressed, and went back to Nashville the following day. I saw Brenda a few more times, once after she married the actor Corbin Bernsen, when they were driving to Los Angeles, but eventually lost touch with both sisters.

That September I entered Vanderbilt, and with my year's worth of credits I managed to take mostly sophomore classes, trying to fit myself into a program where I was already two or three years older than my classmates. I was not only older, however, but far more experienced, not to mention eccentric, than the other students. I had no interest in the social aspects of college, which made it impossible for me to feel a part of the community, and I don't think I spoke more than ten words a day for the entire academic year. I liked my studies, particularly a creative writing class, which was taught by Walter Sullivan, a brilliant writer himself, and while I found a mild sense of camaraderie there, I still made no real friends.

A few months into the school year I moved out of my dad's house, having found an apartment on Seventeenth Avenue South, at the back of an old building (which, ironically, I would buy six years later when I was married to Rodney Crowell and we needed office space on Music Row). Steve Scruggs, Randy's younger brother, started coming by my place in the evenings, a few times a week, with his guitar. He usually showed up around nine o'clock, fidgety and distracted, talkative and achingly lonely. He played me songs he was working on, and I played him some of my own. By this time I had become serious about songwriting myself, and wanted desperately to break through to a level of craft that I worshipped in the songs of Guy Clark, Mickey Newbury, Townes Van Zandt, and Rodney Crowell. I had not yet written a good song. Steve was a sweet friend, and if he had romantic motives when he visited me, he never let on, and we became very comfortable passing the guitar back and forth on those quiet nights.

Twenty-five years after moving to London, in October of 2001, I sat at my father's bedside in the intensive care unit of a hospital in Nashville. He had just narrowly escaped death for the fifth or sixth time over the preceding several years. His precarious health was a constant and exhausting drama of acute and sudden illnesses followed by near-miraculous recoveries, and this latest medical catastrophe had left him jittery and depleted. I sat quietly holding his hand while he ran through his repertoire of tics—jerking, trembling, murmuring. Trying to think of something to engage his attention, I finally said, "I'm writing a book, Dad."

He harrumphed, emphatically—one of the peculiar ways he liked to communicate.

I described one of the chapters to him: I am sitting on a beach, in Jamaica, staring at the sky and letting the tidal pull of my own future wash over me and draw me forward. I am full of my unlived life, and the joy of anticipation for it is taking me apart, cell by cell, and putting me back together in ways that could accommodate a thousand potentials. I am certain to outgrow myself. I can feel it all coming for me, and I am running to meet it in my deepest heart, in London.

I was deliberately eloquent for him, describing my feelings in detail, the anticipation and the smell of the sea in the darkness, the brightness of the stars, my young, smooth feet in the sand, and the two silent boys at my side, like gargoyles protecting my dream.

He grew still and stared straight ahead through the glass doors to the nurse's station while I talked. When I finished, he turned to me with surprise.

"You got me. With that chapter." He thought for a moment. "I didn't know you felt all those things then."

Neither of us spoke for a moment or two; then softly I said, "Well, I did."

Dad's eyes glazed a bit, and he said quietly, "Just to think of you makes my heart swell with pride."

Randy Scruggs married in April of 1976. He and Sandy are still married and have one daughter, Lindsey. He is a successful record producer, musician, and songwriter and owns his own production company and studio in Nashville. We renewed our friendship in our late twenties and have worked together many times. When I recorded my dad's old song "Tennessee Flat-Top Box" in 1987, it became a number one hit, with Randy playing the signature guitar line.

I saw our dear friend John Rollins for the last time on New Year's Eve 2000, at Cinnamon Hill, when I was there to see in the new millennium with my husband, John, and our baby, Jake. As John Rollins walked out of the house into the balmy evening, wearing his pink golf shirt and white trousers and wishing everyone a happy new year, I said good-bye to him and thought to myself very clearly, *This is the last time I will ever see him*. He died of a heart attack while taking his afternoon nap that spring, in his offices in Wilmington, Delaware.

Ted Rollins became estranged from his father for many years, and reconciled with him a few years before John died. Ted is still very close to our family and was particularly close to my father. He always made Dad laugh. When Dad was confined to a wheelchair in the last year of his life, Ted came over with silver paint pens and drew rocket ships and explosions all over the chair. He has become like a brother to me.

Brenda Cooper became a successful and respected Emmy Award–winning fashion stylist for television and film. We reconnected when she divorced and moved back to New York. The first time I appeared on David Letterman's show, she accompanied me to allay my nervousness. Before the taping, we were in my dressing room with the door open when Letterman himself walked by. Brenda leaped from her chair and accosted him, shrieking, "You had better be nice to her!" Letterman was so taken with her animation, upper-crust accent, and striking looks that toward the end of my televised segment he called her out onstage. She took a seat next to me, and when he asked her if he had passed muster, she giggled and told him that he had indeed.

Sandy moved to New York, where I lost track of her. I think of her still.

Steve Scruggs committed suicide on September 13, 1992.

While writing this account, I received an e-mail from David, the son of the head of the British fan club for my dad who had so kindly appeared at the airport when I had first arrived in England and whose invitations to dinner I had never accepted. David had found me on the Internet and wrote to me, thinking that I would want to know that his father had just died.

Maurice Oberstein went on to have an illustrious career and was always respected as a gentleman in an ungentlemanly business. After his tenure as managing director at Columbia Records UK, he moved on to become CEO of Polygram International. He is credited with being one of the chief architects of the modern British recording industry. He died of leukemia in London on August 12, 2001, at the age of seventy-two.

In January 2007, I was in Sydney, Australia, playing at the State Theatre. When I arrived in my dressing room, I found a note from Derek Witt: "Remember me? We worked together." I had not heard from him since 1977, so I called him when I was in London the following month. He had long since left the music business, and we had a nice long chat. He later sent me his photograph with an accompanying note that said, "I'm very happy with my lot in life." Later that year, in November, the night before I was scheduled for brain surgery, I got a message on my cell phone that Derek had died.

Malcolm Eade is currently the vice president of international A&R for Epic Records UK. He is happily married with three children and is a grandfather. In our first phone call after twenty-six years, which left me in tears, he said to me, "I remember everything about you."

Anthea Joseph died on Christmas Eve 1997 at the age of fifty-seven. She had been living alone with her two cats in the countryside outside London. She had ended her professional life in the music business as personal assistant to Obie at Polygram.

In 2009, my youngest daughter, Carrie, went to London for a short visit. She called me from Hampstead to ask me the exact address where I had lived, and then an hour later she e-mailed me a photo of herself, twenty years old, as I had been, standing in front of No. 3 Carlingford Road. A chill went through me; it was like looking at a photo of a time traveler who arrived where her mother had begun, with all the beauty, circumspection, and grace that I had longed for, and strained to glimpse.

Today, I can't sit on a beach and look at the moon without realizing that my life is more than half over, and that the same moon that reproaches me now with my unlived dreams once drew me across the ocean with mysterious promises. My life was changed utterly by my six months in London. I often think that perhaps I didn't stay long enough, but I've forgiven Dad for making me come home. It makes my heart swell just to think of it.

The word "contrition" comes from the Latin word for "bruise" or "grind," a derivation that makes perfect sense to me as a former Catholic. Something in the drone and the rhythm of the Act of Contrition—"*Through my fault, through my most grievous fault . . . ,*" which I said to a man behind a screen in a dark confessional booth for so many years—was uniquely compelling. It took me many years to realize it wasn't my fault, or even my grievous fault, however much I was drawn in by the swing of the words and the safe intimacy of confession. What all those anxiously droned Acts of Contrition chiefly accomplished was to break me down, bruising my sense of self permanently. Or so I thought. In any case, they had the immediate effect of making me withdraw from the truth about myself for a very long time. The truth about me, as it turned out, was unacceptable not only to Catholicism but to adults in general. The truth about me was not meant to fit into the system of convent school, religion, contrition, or punition. None of that mattered. I was a writer. It would save me.

One day in 1990, after I had finished my album *Interiors* and was beginning to write the songs for *The Wheel,* I went to my file cabinet and aimlessly pulled out a folder of papers my mother had recently sent me of my artwork, homework, and spelling lists from the seventh grade. Leafing through them I came upon an English project I had done on metaphors and similes. Reading the piece, I vividly remembered the excitement I had felt on being given this particular assignment, for it was the very first time in my entire career as a student that I had been excited about anything the nuns had ever asked me to do. I read through my discussion of metaphors and similes, and I could feel the thrill of my twelve-year-old self coming off the page, a nascent writer in love with language as if language were a potential lover. I came to a single page that said, in big letters I had printed very, very carefully, "A lonely road is a bodyguard." It was a metaphor I had invented, and I was pleased with myself for having chosen this powerful image over the more straightforward simile, "A lonely road is *like* a bodyguard." I lifted that sentence from my seventh-grade project and put it directly into a song I was writing, "Sleeping in Paris":

> *I'll send the angels to watch over you tonight*
> *And you send them right back to me.*
> *A lonely road is a bodyguard*
> *If you really want it to be.*

That song ended up on *The Wheel,* and whenever I hear it now, or think of it, or sing it, I nod to my little girl self, and she, in the wisdom of her great distance and perspective, looks on with pleasure and the patience of one who has waited a long time to be noticed. This one line, in this one song, is how I know who I am, and how I know I survived.

When I became a student at Vanderbilt in 1976, I declared a double major in English and drama, but I quickly discovered I could not break into the clique of drama students who got cast in plays because I was quiet, extremely shy, and a bit overweight. I also lacked any of the vibrancy or ambition that would have caught the attention of the teacher, whom I found somewhat distant and pontificating anyway. Two other professors, however, did make a great impact on me: Dr. Reba Wilcoxon, a tough and insightful English teacher who gave me the assignment to write a Menippean satire, which was one of the most memorable and exciting writing experiments of my life, and the great Walter Sullivan, eminent professor, authority on Southern literature (particularly the fugitive and agrarian movements), and a wonderfully lyrical author and teacher. When I arrived at Vanderbilt, he had been teaching there for twenty-seven years and went on to teach for twenty-three more, retiring in 2000. In his youth he had been part of a young writers group that included Flannery O'Connor, Eudora Welty, and Robert Penn Warren. He was deeply inspiring in his gentle incisiveness, taking my terrible, saccharine, and sophomoric stories seriously, and encouraging me again and again to write "what I know."

I loved his class, and he made me feel not only important but that I might actually have a future in writing. It was a promise that had been waiting for fulfillment—waiting since I was nine years old and won a poetry contest at school, waiting since I'd had the imaginative daring to conceive of a road as a bodyguard. But despite Professor Sullivan's mentoring, Vanderbilt just didn't work. I wasn't a college girl. I was odd, removed, quiet, intensely lonely, and prone to living inside my own thoughts, often to my detriment and deep emotional disturbance. I didn't care about the school at all, and lacking any of the natural enthusiasm of young women my age, I had no desire to socialize with my classmates. I wanted to be a writer, but becoming a good writer seemed an insurmountable and confusing task.

After finishing the academic year, I decided to move back to Los Angeles, where I enrolled in the Lee Strasberg Theatre Institute. I was impatient with myself as a writer. I couldn't see that I was getting better, so I thought I would try acting. I got an apartment on Fuller Avenue in Hollywood, close to the Institute, which was on Hollywood Boulevard at Highland Avenue. My father continued to subsidize me, paying my rent—$345 a month, an exorbitant amount in 1977—tuition, and living expenses.

I took to Method acting classes like a duck to water. I spent all day and evening, every day, at the Institute, I read Stanislavski as if it were the Bible, I watched the single existing film of Eleanora Duse, who was revered by Method actors, as if it held the key to all mysteries, and for six months I lived and breathed "The Work" with absolute and fierce focus. I was a Method elitist, and everything outside of the Institute appeared meaningless and colorless to me. I audited the classes that Strasberg—whom we were all encouraged to casually address as Lee—taught, but he scared me (and everyone else in the program) to death. He was brutal in his feedback, which he often used manipulatively. He might effusively praise an actor after a scene one week and completely ignore her the next, or spend an hour humiliating someone and then only casually remark "Nice work" to the other actor in the same scene. No one could predict his moods or understand his motives.

My own acting teacher, Dominic DeFazio, was an intense Italian who was also ruthless in his assessments of his students, but while he was tough he was also encouraging. I quickly developed an enormous crush on him, which I could barely conceal, leaving me flustered and frozen around him. But I wanted to learn, and the exercises he taught us for accessing buried emotion and for connecting the feelings to external content were enormously helpful to me in my personal life, and became even more useful later on, when I became a performer.

One scene I did for Dominic required me to cry on cue, and after weeks of rehearsal I was still consumed with anxiety about my ability to accomplish it. On the day of the scene I stood in the wings before going onstage in the classroom, absolutely petrified and certain that I would be unable even to walk out onto the stage. But I did go on, and when I got to the point in the scene where I was supposed to cry, I was delighted to find that my training had worked, and I produced the requisite tears. I then discovered, however, that I couldn't stop, and I cried through the rest of the twenty-minute scene. At the end of it I took my chair in the center of the stage next to the other actor to wait for Dominic's feedback. He paused and then said dryly, "Rosanne, your fee for films just went up to a million dollars." I couldn't have been more pleased with myself; after growing up as the girl who never cried, I was now the girl who couldn't stop crying, albeit once removed from reality.

Within a few weeks I had made a number of friends at the Institute, something that didn't happen in an entire year at Vanderbilt. Nadejda Klein, who was married to my dad's agent, Marty Klein, at Agency for the Performing Arts, was a dark, sophisticated beauty with two children and a fantastic Eastern European accent. I copied her in almost everything—the way she dressed, her affectations, and her extralong More cigarettes, even though cigarettes held no appeal for me at all. I spent a lot of time with Nadejda, eating exotic lunches and, of course, fervently discussing The Work and our mutual obsession with the Duse film.

The first day of my cold-reading class, I took a seat on a bench outside the room where the session was shortly to begin. Next to me was a tall, beautiful girl about my age I had never seen before. We were both anxious, as the teacher was known to be tough, and cold reading allowed not only no preparation but myriad opportunities for humiliation. Suddenly, in the tense silence between us on the bench, the girl burst into tears. I reached out and took her hand, and we became friends from that moment on. She introduced herself as Kelly McGillis.

Another of my fellow students got a job in the television series *Columbo*, and it so happened that the episode for which he was hired, "Swan Song," starred my dad as a traveling evangelist who kills his wife, played by Ida Lupino. After filming his scene, my friend told me that he had played a mechanic who was meant to be nervous and awestruck upon meeting my dad's character. When I asked him what motivation he used to create the nervous excitement—the classic acting school question—he sheepishly replied, "I just used meeting Johnny Cash."

It was, all things considered, a strange time in my life. A serial killer, the Hillside Strangler, was then on the loose in Los Angeles. My mother, seventy miles north in Ventura, was beside herself with continuous worry over me, with good cause. I sometimes left the Institute at eleven p.m. and walked obliviously into the dark, empty parking lot alone. Men followed me home from the supermarket. My apartment was broken into twice; the second time, all my jewelry was stolen, which devastated me. I told my father, who sent me a new piece of jewelry every week for several weeks. A pair of pearl earrings would be accompanied by a note saying, "My love is more precious than pearl earrings." He got as far as "My love is more precious than Cartier watches" before he finally stopped. I still wear the Cartier Tank watch he gave me in that marathon of generosity.

I had affairs with a couple of fellow actors, neither of whom I felt particularly drawn to, but I thought it was something I was supposed to do. I was so desperately trying to find my real life, but I was frustrated and out of focus. I loved the class work at the Institute, but I had not gone out on a single audition, which most of the other students in the school were doing regularly. I started asking myself hard questions about being an actor: Was I just in love with the insulation the Institute afforded and the privileged, almost cultlike experience of being under the auspices of Lee Strasberg? Was my skin really thick enough for me to go out on auditions and get rejected over and over again? I knew in my heart that being part of a group of people who were singularly committed to an artistic ideal mesmerized me, but I recognized that I could not make a life as an actor. I could not bring myself to go on auditions, and the idea of drawing so much attention to my physical appearance, a significant part of getting a job, was absolutely horrifying. I was already obsessed with the worry that I had the wrong kind of nose to be a great actress. After comparing my small ski-slope nose with that of every actress I could think of, I found that not a single one shared my exact shape, which I interpreted as a fundamental indication of my lack of acting ability.

By December of 1977, I was floundering. The spell of The Work was wearing off, and I was a little panicked about my next move. I decided to get as far away from Los Angeles as I could, and I arranged to visit my dad's friend Renate Damm in Germany for several weeks over the holiday break.

I arrived in cold Munich in early December and moved into the tiny spare bedroom of Renate's apartment in the Siegfriedstrasse, near the English Gardens. I only knew Renate from touring in Europe with Dad and June, as she was the international liaison for their record label and always traveled with them. Dad had made the call to Renate to ask if she would host me for a short while, and she was incredibly gracious and welcoming. A decade older than me, she treated me like a beloved little sister. Her birthday was December 12, which was just a day or two after I appeared, and that night we went to a huge party for her at Ariola Records, the label where she worked. There I met many of her colleagues, and Renate told them all that I was an excellent songwriter. At this point I had written a dozen or so songs, most of them perfectly awful. One of the heads of the A&R department said to me, very seriously, that if I was to make a demo of them and send them to him, he would consider signing me to Ariola, to make a record to be released only in Europe. I was noncommittal, but I became secretly excited by the idea and later discussed it with Renate at length. After my truncated stay in London, I had been longing to move back to Europe, and quietly making a record in Germany and not having anyone in the States notice it would enable me to avoid any comparisons to my dad. I went back to Los Angeles and, with some trepidation, terminated my enrollment at the Lee Strasberg Institute. That was the end of my formal education.

Someone once told me to perform to the six percent of the audience who are poets. I have this in my mind at some point every time I sing, but I often have to find that six percent by looking past those who are yawning, glazed over, distracted, unsettled; those who come to try to look through me to see my dad; and those who can't respond to music but like the experience of sitting in a crowd with those who can.

Sometimes, onstage, I am also one of those people who are yawning, glazed over, distracted, and unsettled. At some concerts I have felt as transparent as a pane of glass and haven't been able to hear the music I'm making. Sometimes music has been so painful to me that I want nothing more than silence and the sound of waves. Sometimes the need to please the audience rises in me like bile and ruins everything.

T-Bone Burnett, an old friend, once told Joe Henry, "Don't stop working, just stop worrying," advice that Joe passed on to me that has since become my mantra. Now, even when I do worry, I keep working. Work, I remind myself, is redemption.

When the time came to produce four demos to send to Ariola, I called Rodney Crowell. I had met him only once, at a party at Waylon Jennings's house in 1976, when I was still attending Vanderbilt. He was at the party with Emmylou Harris, her husband and producer, Brian Ahern, and his old friend and recording engineer Donivan Cowart. That night, when everyone started passing the guitar around, Rodney and Donivan played a song they had just written called "Leaving Louisiana in the Broad Daylight." I was stunned. I thought it was just about the best song I had ever heard, and perversely my heart sank. Writing a song that good seemed so far out of my reach that I felt like giving up my dream of songwriting. I was rattled, and even a bit despairing. Susanna and Guy Clark, longtime friends of Rodney's, were also at the party, and at some point in the evening Susanna introduced me to Rodney. He didn't really seem to notice me, but I was riveted by him. Rodney had also written what I considered a definitive, world-class ballad, "'Til I Gain Control Again," and he played rhythm guitar in Emmylou's band. I had gone to see Emmylou at the Hammersmith Odeon when I lived in London and had taken note of the cute, lanky rhythm guitarist, never imagining that six months later I would be sitting in Waylon Jennings's living room hearing him sing a new composition, and falling hard for him in the process.

I thought his particular sensibility would be perfect for what I wanted to do with my demos. I also thought it would be a way to get to know him and try to get him to like me. I don't think I even understood what it meant to be a producer—I just knew he was a great songwriter and that if he could write those songs, we probably shared a similar musical aesthetic, or at least an aesthetic I could aspire to, and he could produce four songs for me. Years later, he always gave me credit for making him a record producer. When I called him, he said apologetically that he had never produced anything before. I told him that experience didn't matter and that I knew he could do it, so we made plans to meet in Nashville, where he was living with his wife, Martha, and baby, Hannah. I was even more attracted to him after that first preproduction meeting. I remember telling June of my inner struggle over my growing fixation on him after we had met a number of times to work. When I asked her advice, she merely sighed and said, "Honey, if he's married, it will never work. Just forget about it." Odd advice, perhaps, given what had happened between her and my dad, but I tried to take it and to forget about Rodney. After the demos were finished, I sent them to Ariola, and they were pleased enough with the results that they offered me a recording contract, for the European market only.

Just before I left Los Angeles for Munich to begin the Ariola record, Renate came to see me. After we met with the lawyers who wrote up my contract, we made some social calls. Renate had made a point of introducing me to a wide variety of music when I lived with her in Munich. I'd seen Billy Joel at the beginning of his career, alone at a piano in a bar with only a few hundred people in the audience. I'd seen Bette Midler when she was first playing her character Delores DeLago, the mermaid in a wheelchair. (Some of the subtle, twisted humor was lost on the Germans, and I remember laughing louder than anyone in the audience.) But mostly we'd gone to hear jazz, as Renate was obsessed with it. I didn't really get jazz, and it would be another decade before I came to appreciate it, but in retrospect that first introduction I got to jazz in Germany was very important, for I filed it somewhere in my mind until I had more life and musical experience to apply to the experience of listening to it.

Renate had a number of friends in Los Angeles who were in the jazz world, among them Herbie and Gigi Hancock and Jon and Maria Lucien. We went to Herbie and Gigi's house one evening for dinner, and I was very quiet throughout—I felt at a loss to say anything intelligent or interesting to Herbie Hancock, who intimidated me completely. Renate started telling Herbie about my songs and how I was just about to make my first record. Then she asked if he would like to hear my demos, as she happened to have the tape in her purse. I was absolutely mortified and, flushing, protested, but Renate insisted. Herbie graciously accepted the invitation and after dinner settled back on his sofa while Renate put on the tape. He listened thoughtfully and nodded at me. "There's something about your voice," he said. Then he added, "Country music. I could get into that." I let out a breath of relief, thinking, *At least he didn't seem to hate it.* I begged Renate not to play it for Jon Lucien, and fortunately he was not there on our visit to his home, so we had a brief visit with Maria only. While I had no confidence in my vocal abilities at that time and very little in my songwriting, Renate's lavish praise and encouragement, as well as her talking me up to everyone she came across, helped me develop at least a bit of assurance.

I wanted Rodney to produce the album, but Ariola was adamant that I record in Munich with a staff producer, Bernie Vonficht. So I returned to Munich and moved back in with Renate, and plans began for recording.

A few days before we were scheduled to go into the studio, I found myself unable to get out of bed. I couldn't seem to get enough sleep, and when I was awake, I couldn't think clearly. After a couple of days of this, Renate became alarmed and insisted on taking me to a doctor. "What's wrong with her?" Renate asked, once he had posed a few questions and examined me. "She's depressed," the doctor said abruptly, and that was the end of the consultation. As he ushered us out, I began to accept the fact that I wasn't entirely sure I even wanted to make a record. I had, I knew, been carefully avoiding reconciling myself to undertaking a project that, if successful, could help to make me famous. I wanted success, certainly, but I wanted it without the merciless exposure of a public life. I believed that I could be deeply satisfied and achieve success by becoming a great songwriter, but without being a performer. The idea of performing, of going on endless tours and living the draining, peripatetic life my dad was leading, was not appealing. From a very young age I'd spent enough time behind the curtain to not have any illusions about a performer's life being one of glamour and excitement. The bone-crushing exhaustion, the constant vulnerability to media misinterpretation or even slander, and the complete obliteration of any semblance of a private life were not things I wanted for myself. My native reticence was not attracted to any part of it. But I did want the songs. I wanted to write them and I even wanted to sing them. I wanted to collaborate with other musicians, and construct arrangements and sonic textures and poetry, and get inside a rhythm and a beat, and go into the studio like a painter and create something from nothing. In the end, I wanted to do that so badly that I concluded that the benefits outweighed the attending risks, so I got out of bed and began sessions for my first record in the spring of 1978.

I went into the studio with Bernie and a band he had assembled, and though the first few days went relatively well, Bernie and I soon began to have some differences of opinion. Even though I was young and inexperienced, I had intuitive but very definite ideas about how I wanted to sound and what songs were right for me. My deep respect for great songwriters and my intense feelings about particular songs, songs I knew were pristine examples of true songwriting, were a guiding force in the studio when I found myself over my head and inarticulate about arrangements or sonics. This intuition became sharply focused when, midway through the initial tracking sessions, Bernie brought in a piece he wanted me to record called "Lucky." I hated the song and said, as diplomatically as I could, that it was not right for me and that I didn't want to do it. Bernie was equally adamant and we got into a heated argument, but I held my ground. The next day I showed up at the studio at the regular time to discover that he had called the musicians in an hour earlier to record the instrumental track, hoping that, on hearing it, I would capitulate and add my vocals. I refused again. He began shouting that the song would be a hit, and that if I wouldn't record it, he would sing it himself. I told him to be my guest.

(Several months later, when the record was finished and released and I had gone back to Europe to promote it, I shared the pressrooms and television shows with another new artist and former record producer, Bernie Vonficht, who had had an enormous hit with a song called "Lucky," as he had foreseen. Bernie looked at me warily in the pressrooms, as if embarrassed by his success, but I was genuinely glad for him. I wouldn't have recorded the song even if I had known it would sell triple platinum. I knew I'd have to sing it for the rest of my life, and it wasn't worth it.)

While making the record, I tried to forge friendships with some expatriate musicians who were working in the club and studio scene in Munich, but they all seemed to be so lonely. The experience was unsettling for me, for I had been thinking of moving to Germany and trying to make a living as they did, but the longer I was there the more frightened I became of the isolation I might encounter. I did become close with a woman named Lucy Neale, a dedicated roots-type songwriter who paid her bills by dancing and singing with a disco group. She was as talented as she was sweet, but a few years later she went back to San Diego to sell real estate. I am certain I would have had a similar trajectory if I had stayed in Munich. I still loved hearing music in the clubs and visiting the English Gardens and the outdoor markets, and I liked going to the casinos deep in Bavaria with Renate's rich friends. And if I loved being away from the even starker isolation of Los Angeles, I knew I was still adrift.

After the record was finished, I returned to Los Angeles and waited, uncertain what to do with myself. One song, called "Thoughts from the Train," which was cowritten by Lucy and Israeli pop star Igal Bashan, was getting some radio play in Germany, but it was not even close to being a hit, and it appeared that my recording career might be over shortly after its inception.

It was at this point that my dad stepped in, without my knowing it. One afternoon at his house on the lake, he had a meeting with

Rick Blackburn, the head of Columbia Records in Nashville. As the meeting wound down, Dad said, "Listen to this record my daughter Rosanne made," and put my eponymous Ariola album on the turntable. Rick told me later that he didn't like what he was hearing at all, but halfway through that first song the phone rang and Dad left the room to take the call. Rick got up and put the needle on a different track, which captivated him immediately. When Dad came back, Rick impulsively told him that he was going to offer me a recording contract. Dad never told me the story himself, and if Rick hadn't related it to me when he signed me, I would never have known how I came to be offered a contract with Columbia Records. I didn't tell this story for another twenty years, as I didn't want anyone to think I had gotten a recording contract only because of my dad's influence.

My life started to change drastically. I was off the horrible hormone shots, and my weight had returned to normal, along with a more airy and ebullient sense of self. My relationship with Rodney, who had divorced, had become a romance, and we had begun talking about marriage. His own first record, *Ain't Livin' Long Like This*, had just come out, but he went back to Germany with me to do a little promotion for the Ariola album. During that trip I received an offer to do a midday show in an enormous circuslike tent with a few other artists in the countryside outside Munich, to be broadcast live over Radio Luxembourg. Ariola was adamant about the importance of this appearance, and they guaranteed an audience of five thousand people. I briefly wondered how they expected to get five thousand people into a tent in a rural area at noon on a weekday, but I pushed the thought aside. After a long drive into Bavaria, my car pulled up behind the tent and I was alarmed to see animals—circus animals— being led around by trainers. My heart jumped into my throat; what exactly had I agreed to?

I got out of the car and peeked into the tent, where approximately ninety people were seated in the bleachers of the vast space and a few animals were milling listlessly around the perimeter. Then the producer of the show explained to me, "You will walk to the center ring when they introduce you and you will lip-synch your song." *Lip-synch?* I was dumbfounded. I asked, "What's the point? If you're just playing the record, why do you need me here?" He gestured to the audience. The ninety people had come to see *me*.

When I was introduced and walked glumly to the center ring, all ninety people swarmed the stage. I swallowed my humiliation and told myself I could do anything for three minutes; I had been scheduled for only one song. Here, on the German country circus circuit, lip-synching on Radio Luxembourg, I was a rock star. Here was my official entrée into a performing life of my own.

Thirty-one years later, in March of 2009, I returned to perform a concert in Munich—oddly enough, for the very first time. I spent two days catching up with Renate, who I had only seen a few times in the last three decades, and who fell easily into her old role of solicitous big sister on the day of the show, finding the right tea, arranging for taxis, practicing my meager German with me, and translating for the crew. It was an acoustic show, with just my husband, John, and me at the Muffathalle, a cavernous old hall. The event was sublime, with the small crowd of only a few hundred people feeling as close as family. It felt like a long-awaited reunion, with all the emotional depth of loss and redemption, youth and maturity, beginnings and endings. I had asked Renate to invite Bernie Vonficht to the show, and the three of us were in tears afterward. Bernie said that he had become deeply disillusioned with the music business and allowed that the choice I'd made at the time not to record "Lucky" was "good for you, and good for me." A circle in my life became complete that night. If the young girl who was me in 1978 had known that over the next thirty-one years she would gain some real mastery over the things she most longed to express, if she could have been at the show at the Muffathalle in 2009 and felt the air buzzing with the chemical connection that can form between performer and audience, she could have saved herself a trip to the doctor before that first recording session, and many years of doubt and uncertainty afterward.

Many nights have passed and many miles have been traveled between the circus tent and the Muffathalle, and thousands of dirty clubs and late shows, bone-rattling buses and grimy motels, and dressing rooms that smelled of piss and cigarettes. There have been nights of sitting backstage and staring at a face in the mirror exhausted to the point of being unrecognizable, and endless airport hallways I've walked at dawn, with a paper cup of milky lukewarm tea and a painful sense of longing for home. There have been audiences who were curious, restrained, drunk, ebullient, resentful, respectful, there to defend my dad's honor or to try to catch a glimpse of him in my voice or face, or almost entirely absent. But through all of it, I worked hard, I paid attention, I sang to the six percent even if only two percent showed up on a given night, I sang to become better, I sang for the band if no one else was listening, I just kept doing it until it felt like home. I worked out a lifetime of self-doubt and musical and emotional vulnerabilities under the spotlight. Performing has been an enormous gift, cloaked at first in a mantle of risk and suspicion, only to reveal itself as the treasure I couldn't even define in 1978. The arena I thought was a circus tent of humiliation actually held half the available light of what was intended for me, for my whole life.

When the time came to record my album for Columbia, they agreed to let Rodney produce it. In February of 1979, we returned to Los Angeles to begin work. He had quit Emmylou's band to make his own first record, but he quickly diverted his attention from the promotion of that record to the production of mine. We effectively adopted and slipped comfortably into the recording style, work ethic, and camp of the musicians surrounding Emmylou and Brian. Rodney hired Emory Gordy, Jr., to play bass, Tony Brown to play piano, John Ware on drums, Frank Reckard on guitar, and Hank DeVito to play steel guitar on the basic tracks. Hank was also a great friend and advisor duiring those first sessions. Later we added Ricky Skaggs, Albert Lee, Hal Blaine, and James Burton, as well as Emmylou and the Whites on background vocals.

We began recording at the Enactron Truck, Brian's mobile recording facility, which was parked at a big, empty house on Lania Lane in Beverly Hills, just off Mulholland Drive. The artists, musicians, and hangers-on who came through there, and the late nights and the craziness—not to mention the great music created in the truck—became the stuff of legend. Brian himself was an almost mythic figure to me, and I had fantasies of Rodney and I becoming a creative duo of the same stature and originality as he and Emmylou.

Brian could be mercurial and moody, but I had a deep affection and respect for him. (When Emmy and Brian broke up and she moved to Nashville, I feared that I might lose contact with Brian completely, and that almost proved to be true. I didn't see him for another twenty years or so, until I was singing on a Maura O'Connell record that was being recorded in the Enactron Truck, which Brian still owned and by now had been moved to Nashville.)

Working in the Enactron Truck was like being in a submarine. Brian had a great old Neve recording console in there, and the sound was spectacular. During the recording sessions we set up the band to record the tracks inside the house—in the kitchen, bedrooms, and even the bathroom, which had a great natural reverb—and sometimes around the swimming pool, for the ambient echo. We did some overdubs inside the cramped truck, but most of the recording was remote. (The house itself on Lania Lane was more than a little unsettling, as a murder had been committed there. A young man had gone crazy and killed his entire family, and as no one subsequently wanted to buy it, Brian was able to rent the empty dwelling for recording. Occasionally, late at night, when only Rodney and I were there with an engineer doing overdubs, I was overcome by a creepy feeling and refused to go into the house alone.)

Rodney and I got married in the middle of mixing the record, and we delayed our honeymoon to Hawaii by three weeks in order to finish and master it. When I think about making that album, I am struck mostly by how young I was at the time—twenty-three years old—and how I had attitude but no confidence, passion but very little real focus. I learned a lot during the process: I learned how to listen to drums, I learned some breath control and how to sustain a note, and I learned about the layered process of recording—the basic tracks, the overdubs, the mixing, and the mastering. This precise sequence of events and the intricacies of recording itself had eluded me during the making of the Ariola record, as I had been operating from a defensive posture and wary of asking questions or appearing vulnerable. This was different; I now had a great deal at stake. I wanted to be certain not only that I created music true to who I was, but also that I understood exactly how I could achieve that technically.

In the late 1970s record making was like creating a sculpture or a painting. There was a lot of kinesthetic information, beyond the sonic, in the studio. Air and magnetic tape were the quintessential elements of the craft of analog recording. A recording console that was as big as a Volkswagen had to be turned on and warmed up, and lights and knobs and faders were manipulated to record and design music. Obsessive attention was paid to exactly where microphones were placed and how far away they were from the instruments. (In the late seventies and early eighties it was fashionable to place six or eight microphones around a drum kit to record every nuance of every beat. I was shocked when I went to sing a guest vocal on a record produced by the legendary Glyn Johns and saw that he had *one* microphone hanging above the drum kit. Rodney and I rethought our entire approach to recording after that experience.)

Big tape machines whirred in the back of the control room to capture what was coming through the board, and if you did too many overdubs or ran the tape too many times, tiny, almost microscopic flecks of iron oxide would start to flake off. (The horror story—probably apocryphal—making the rounds of Los Angeles studios at that time concerned Fleetwood Mac's *Tusk*, which was released later that year. Engineer had told engineer until everyone in the recording industry had heard that they had run the tape so many times, for hundreds upon hundreds of overdubs and edits, that they were having to mop up little piles of oxide from the machine every day and that actual sonic holes were becoming noticeable in the tracks. We were thrilled by this cautionary tale, and I became obsessed with *not* running the tape.) Splicing tape was a technically exact art, and whenever we did edits I would hang over the engineer—in the early days, it was always Donivan Cowart or Bradley Hartman—and hold my breath while he twisted the reels back and forth until finding the tiny opening between notes to take a razor and cut the tape. "Come on. You could drive a truck through that space," I'd encourage him.

There was no such thing as automation, so mixing was a "live" event, with everyone's hands on the board. Brad took the rhythm section, Rodney took the guitars and keyboards, Donivan kept a close eye on the fades and tape speed, and I handled the vocals. We each rode our individual faders with held breath. Oftentimes, two of us would have a great mix and the third would need another take. Mixing went on for endless days and nights, and we often got to bed at six in the morning and started work again at two the next afternoon. I took engineering manuals home with me to study, thinking that in the future I wanted to write, record, and mix my own records, just as a painter might create a solo painting on canvas.

When we finished mixing, we took the tapes to the mastering lab. A vinyl "mother," the prototype of the LPs that would be pressed, was created from the half-inch master, which in turn had been created from the two-inch 24-track tape. An initial pressing of twenty-five thousand records was made from that mother. I went to the lab and stood by the lathe as it cut my mastered record, and then we took it home to listen. (We mastered *Seven Year Ache*, my second album for Columbia, a few days after John Lennon was murdered, and I asked the mastering engineer to scratch a message—"Goodbye, John"—into the run-out groove of the mother vinyl. Now, whenever someone brings a vinyl LP of *Seven Year Ache* to a concert for me to sign, I always look at the run-out groove to see if it's one of the original twenty-five thousand copies, and if the message is there. I've seen only one in all this time. I know Hank DeVito has a copy, but mine is lost.)

The entire process, start to finish, felt like a handcrafted work—turning knobs, pushing colored buttons, cutting tape, and making deep grooves into vinyl. The art and process of making records remained substantially that way until the advent of digital recording, when the language completely changed and the learning curve became very steep for me. I miss analog recording—the real start-to-finish process, not as a retro nod, as some people do on their way to digital—and the feeling of being so intimately connected to the experience.

We called the album *Right or Wrong*, after the Keith Sykes song that was one of the tracks, and the cover photograph showed me sitting on a coffee table with a small tumbler of red wine at hand. It was an honest photo. No stylist or art director had taken over with their own vision: It was just me, in my own clothes, at the end of a night of recording, with my regular hairstyle and my own glass of wine, which the photographer had given me when I got to her studio. It seems almost like a radical idea today. The record generated one hit—a duet with Bobby Bare on a song written by Rodney called "No Memories Hangin' 'Round," which reached number 11 on the country charts. It was a valiant effort, and had some of the insouciance and bravado that was part of my nature at the age of twenty-three—and also the vulnerability, doubt, and self-consciousness. The only misstep was a cover of my dad's "Big River," which in hindsight I realize a woman has no business recording. That song is the definitive widescreen depiction of the male chase, fueled by the testosterone that underpins so much of great early Delta rock and roll. But even that misstep, in its own way, was truthful.

I had my first baby, Caitlin Rivers Crowell—the "Rivers" for my dad's mother's maiden name—shortly after *Right or Wrong* was released. (She was born at seven a.m., weighing seven pounds, seven ounces, and when she was about seven months old I began recording my second Columbia album, whose centerpiece was my song "Seven Year Ache.") She was a dark-eyed, tiny beauty whom we called "Baby Elvis" because of her wild shock of black hair. I was overcome with emotion on becoming a mother, and shocked at how quickly, and permanently, my worldview changed. I was stunned to find how territorial I felt, how flooded with love and fear for the baby's safety. I had been a free spirit, a nomad, someone who went back and forth to Europe constantly, who mixed records until six in the morning and liked to hang with the guys in the band. Suddenly I was walking a colicky baby in the middle of the night, obsessed about every burp and wheeze and cry. I adored my new baby Caitlin, but I didn't have a clue about how to balance being a mother of an infant and a four-year-old stepdaughter with the demands of making and promoting records. My anxiety levels were off the charts. I was twenty-four years old when we made *Seven Year Ache*, and I was completely unprepared for the attention it would attract or the work expected of me as a result. I considered quitting—giving up making records—because I couldn't envision how to manage my career and motherhood, and do either one reasonably well.

We recorded *Seven Year Ache* in North Hollywood in late 1980, with Albert Lee, Emory Gordy, Jr., Hank DeVito, and John Ware in the band. Rodney was by now in his element as a producer, and the album was an intensely collaborative experience. I remember there being a video game in the studio, *Space Invaders*—the first such game I had ever seen—and I logged countless hours on it in the downtime between recording tracks as an antidote to anxiety. The first single was the title song—probably the best song I had written up to that point—and it was a huge hit, reaching number one in the country charts the week of my twenty-fifth birthday and crossing over to the pop charts, where it reached number 22. The album also eventually rose to number one in the country charts, and two more number one singles followed from it—"Blue Moon with Heartache," also my own song, and "My Baby Thinks He's a Train," written by Leroy Preston.

During this entire period I felt a constant slow burn of panic; I just didn't know how to manage it all. The first television show I did after Caitlin's birth, about the time I began recording *Seven Year Ache*, was a big Nashville variety program featuring a lot of stars, and I flew there from Los Angeles with Caitlin, who was seven months old. I was still carrying some extra baby weight, so I decided to wear a jacket by a wild Japanese clothing designer, which I thought would deflect attention from the ten extra pounds. The jacket was neon pink and made of a parachute-type fabric, with enormous shoulder pads. In Los Angeles, this style was considered avant-garde, but when I walked out onstage at the Opry House, the audience actually laughed at me. The host, Larry Gatlin, bemusedly said something to the effect of "What NFL team do you play for?"

I remember a birthday dinner in New York around the time *Seven Year Ache* came out with some journalists from *Rolling Stone*, a photographer, and various record company people. I didn't have any help with the baby, whom I was holding on my lap in a super-chic restaurant where a baby was totally out of place. Everything began to feel surreal and out of sync. Was I really supposed to quit being a musician now and be a mother? Is that what the anxiety was trying to tell me—that I had to give up something? I didn't want to end my career, but how did a person do both?

That summer, the summer of 1981, I was again pregnant, and Rodney, Hannah, Caitlin, and I moved from our house in Malibu Canyon to a beautiful log house in the woods outside of Nashville. I did not adapt quickly or easily to life in the South. Contrary to what most people thought, I had lived in the South only for a total of seven years of my entire life, and I had no memory of the first three years, having been a baby at the time. I was a California girl, in aesthetic and attitude. After years in Los Angeles, the pace seemed unbearably slow, and I couldn't find a decent bagel or the kind of diapers I liked for Caitlin.

By December and January I was eating nearly a dozen oranges a day. Typically, I eat no more than four oranges a year, as I find them either too tart or too bland—and definitely too watery. It was one of the coldest winters on record, and the house stayed warm until it got down to about fifteen degrees; below that, the beautiful old virgin pine just could not hold the heat. For days on end, as the temperature hovered around zero, sometimes dipping below, we all stayed close to the stone fireplace in the great room. Rodney kept the fire going (a full-time job), and the little girls played quietly with their dolls on a green turn-of-the-century Chinese rug that had been rescued from an old brothel in western Kentucky. I sat in a rocking chair next to them, profile to the fire, a little melancholy, with a bag of oranges on my lap. I ate my way through a new bag each day, tossing the peels into the flames as I rocked. The wild, bitter aroma of singed oranges cut the somber iciness of the room and soothed me. It was my personal statement against the chill. I spent many long days like this.

In the first few days of January, three weeks before my due date, my old friend Randy Scruggs called to ask Rodney and me to participate in a project he was doing with his dad, Earl, and Tom T. Hall. They were making a record called *The Storyteller and the*

*Banjo Man*, and he invited us to come to his studio and sing on a couple of songs. It was around Earl's birthday, and a lot of people planned to be there. At this penultimate phase of gestation, I was past the point of maternal glow, long past being cooed at and patted, and had lately been inspiring only expressions of shock and nervous retreat. But Randy was my dear friend, the record would be finished before I delivered my baby, and I really wanted to sing on it, so I decided to go. I didn't have a coat big enough to close around my belly, and that night turned out to be the coldest one yet of the relentless winter. The air was actually blue when we stepped outside. The thermometer in the carport registered eleven below zero, and sharp little ice crystals rose in gusts from the hard-packed snow in the driveway. I sulked as we started the long drive to the studio. Rodney, experienced with the ramifications of unintentionally provoking a woman near the end of her third trimester, gave me a lot of room. It was a very quiet trip.

Despite my misgivings, the evening turned out to be wonderful. We sang on three songs: "Shackles and Chains," "Roll in My Sweet Baby's Arms," and "Song of the South." Instead of being treated as a sideshow freak, I was cherished as a ripe little goddess. It brought out the best in me. The company of friends and the balm of playing music was liberating, and I was fatigued, but content, when we left. The silence on our return had a decidedly different texture.

We drove through the snowy landscape as if in a dream—past the empty country roads at the borders of wide fields enclosed by Civil War–era stone fences, past big, dark, and looming old estates and grand, columned mansions that lonesomely adjoined lazy suburban tracts.

We had not seen another car for several miles when we made the turn onto the pike that began the final leg to our hidden house in its miniature valley surrounded by thick oaks and maples. Rodney drove very carefully, as this road was used less than others in the area and was still swathed in ice. I was drowsily contemplating a few oranges by the fire before bed. Suddenly, flashing red lights appeared on the shoulder of the opposite side of the road about a hundred feet ahead. We slowed to a crawl, and as we came upon the scene we saw an ambulance, a car behind it, and in between the two, a man stretched out on his back on the frozen ground. The few people standing over him seemed in no hurry to get him into the ambulance.

"Oh, my God," we both said softly when we realized the man was dead. Rodney quickly glanced at me. I turned away, profoundly conscious of the baby inside me, reacting to a fierce, primal impulse to protect it from unexpected surges of my adrenaline—the heady, dangerous mix of the hormones of hysteria and fear.

There was clearly no way we could help, so we drove on. A mile or so farther on, we were astonished to see, striding toward us up the road, a sturdy-looking middle-aged woman with a tall walking stick. Her gait was so determined, and the stick planted so authoritatively with each step, I could practically hear the drumbeat behind her march. More astonishing still, she was dressed only in a skirt and sweater—no coat, scarf, or gloves—and was bare legged. On her feet were awful brown oxford-type discount-store shoes, shaped carelessly from thin, fake leather. Only sandals would have been more inappropriate in this weather.

Rodney stopped and rolled down his window. "Ma'am? Can we give you a ride somewhere?"

In a tight, high-pitched voice she asked, "Are you sure you don't mind?" and then got into the backseat. She was pale and fair, and though her demeanor was reserved, even stiff, her eyes were darting about and she spoke quickly. "Oh, thank you so much! I'm just going back up the road a little bit. My neighbor there called and said someone had been hit by a car, and my husband was out takin' a walk, and now I'm a little worried about him."

I didn't dare look at Rodney, but I could feel that we had both stopped breathing. My heart began to pound, and a queasy feeling rose in my abdomen. Rodney eased the car forward to a little cross street where he could turn around. Fortunately, we didn't have to say anything, because the woman was chattering nervously.

"I told him it was too cold to go out walking, but he's stubborn. Said he had to have his evening constitutional no matter how cold it was. Now, are y'all sure you don't mind takin' me back up there?"

"No, ma'am, not at all," I said. "We saw some kind of disturbance back there, but I'm not sure what it was."

"Oh, my Lord," she trilled, pleading and panicked. "Now, I don't want y'all to get hurt, too!"

I was struck by that sentence as if by a two-by-four. It still reverberates now, so many years later: the pitch of her voice, her self-effacing Southern politeness, the tears building behind the contained panic, the uncontrolled sense that danger newly pervaded the entire world. My heart broke for her. In about thirty seconds her entire life was going to detonate, and two strangers were sharing her last moments of peace. But it was not my place to tell her.

Several years later a friend gave me a tape of Irish keening, which is the sound of women wailing at the graves of their loved ones—long, sustained, unbearably plaintive cries elevated by the deepest sorrow to an art form: the most human sound of the genesis of music. It sent chills down my back and brought tears to my eyes when I heard it, and the first thing I thought of was that woman, unknowing, in her brown plastic shoes.

When we arrived back at her neighbor's house, where the cars and ambulance were still parked, she hurried out of the car. A woman came up to her and put her arm around her shoulder and began to talk softly. We waited for a moment, then drove slowly away. Through the closed car windows I could hear her screams: long, deep, circular cries rising from the roots of her body, like a train whistle disappearing into an endless series of tunnels, like the wrenching Gaelic echoes that hang in the graveyard, like the hiss that escapes from the permanently shattered heart.

I had to borrow from my future that night in protection of my unborn baby. I drew from an unknown reserve of circumspection. *I will feel this later,* I thought. And I was unyielding, my hands over my ears, my head bent to my chest.

On January 25 of that year, I gave birth, after only six hours of labor, to a gorgeous, nearly nine-pound baby girl with enormous bright blue eyes. She was healthy and strong, and I felt proud that I had done my job so well. We named her Chelsea Jane, and I swaddled her warmly and took her home to the big log house. The girls welcomed their little sister and the temperature gradually eased back up into the thirties, where it belonged. My natural indifference to oranges returned abruptly, and the last few left in the bag shriveled and gathered mold before I finally threw them away. I kept the newspaper clipping—"Man Killed by Car on Icy Road"—for a week or so longer, and then that, too, I threw away.

After Chelsea's birth, I was still having things shipped from California, so Rodney and I decided to share a rental apartment in Malibu with Albert Lee and his wife, Karen. Every time I went back to the West Coast, which was fairly regularly, I felt as if I could breathe again. I had not realized how important the ocean was to me, and how suffocating it would feel to live so far from it.

A sweet and placid baby, Chelsea fit in easily with her sisters, who doted on her. The girls were so adorable and funny that I began to take it for granted that they would remain little. I had always pictured myself as the mother of small children, and in my own myopia and self-absorption I couldn't imagine that they would actually grow up and become women. If I had thought more about their development—as well as my own—rather than just reveling at being in the moment with them, I would have been stricter. I would have been diligent about imparting life lessons and establishing regulations and tasks. I would have consciously modeled behavior for them and taught them to cook. They just got me as I was—and that's what they learned about being a woman. In retrospect, I seem to have insisted on a single hard-and-fast rule: no juice after five p.m., as I was convinced that the sugar in the juice would make it difficult to put them to bed. The girls called it "juice cut-off time," and today they tease me mercilessly about it—my one rule.

When I look at my older daughters now, I realize that the women they are today have very little to do with Rodney and me anyway—they became who they were born to be, though their father and I probably contributed a bit to their quirky senses of humor and to their seeing the world in uniquely odd ways. Hannah grew up and moved to Chicago, then San Francisco, then Austin, then briefly came to New York, and then went to Los Angeles. She worked for a time as a nanny, and as a cocktail waitress at the House of Blues. She and I were separated emotionally for a few years, during which time I stayed in touch but not consistently, and I think the space we took from each other helped dissipate the rancor and resentment that had developed in the fraught step-relationship. She was a much better stepdaughter than I was a stepmother. She had equanimity in her native personality, and tremendous inner strength, and acceptance of her situation. I had taken on the job of mothering her at the age of twenty-two, long before I outgrew a need for mothering in myself. I was unprepared and unequipped. She was patient, and long-suffering with my inelegance and sometimes petty attitudes as a stepmother. Hannah has turned out to be a wondrous and humbling gift in my life. She matured into a real beauty—fair and blue eyed like her biological mother, who died when Hannah was twenty-two. She got married in 2004 to a solid young man named Russ Brue, who lived in San Diego and worked in finance. They eventually moved back to Nashville, and Hannah now has two baby girls of her own, as well as a young stepdaughter. She confides in me her difficulties in navigating the stepmother-daughter relationship, and we find a new understanding of each other through that wide circle of relationships. She is a phenomenal mother. She knows things about the domestic arts that I never dreamed of. I feel like a neophyte housewife next to her. She is also preternaturally calm and organized, a woman of grace. I feel safe around her.

Caitlin is much more a type-A personality and for many years led an untamed kind of life. After graduating high school from St. Ann's in Brooklyn, she moved back to Los Angeles, where she worked in the music business, doing song licensing and independent public relations. She is tiny, only five foot three, and very small boned, with big green eyes and a smattering of freckles. (The year after her step-grandmother June died, she did a photo spread for *Elle Girl* magazine, wearing some of June's vintage clothes, and she looked stunning.) I worried about her a lot—she seemed to always live on the edge, taking many physical and emotional risks. She surfed and got heavily tattooed and seemed to relish finding the extremes in everything. (I should have been clued in to her daredevil nature when, at the age of five, she climbed up on a thirty-foot platform at a country club pool and calmly dove off the end.) Then she met a young man, and everything coalesced; the center suddenly began to hold. In 2009, after nine months of courtship, she married Sam Rayner, a young British photographer who is Morrissey's nephew, and moved to Manchester, England. (My friend Elvis Costello said, "In all the connections and interlocking branches of musical family trees, one would never have predicted that one.")

She and Sam laugh at each other constantly and are crazy in love, and with marriage Caitlin has become a fuller, yet more grounded version of who she has always been—a tattooed surfer who is rambunctious and unpredictable, but one who has big, expansive experiences and doesn't play by anyone else's rulebook.

Chelsea is my most unusual child. The tallest of my girls at a not very tall five foot six, Chelsea also developed into a beauty, fair and blue eyed, both elegant and delicate. She has always had an inner life of which I could only catch glimpses, but when she did allow me some knowledge of or access to it, I was introduced to a way of living and of perceiving reality that I had not previously imagined. Once, when she was eleven years old, she tried to explain her understanding of the world to me, and the only thing I could equate it to was some principles of quantum physics, which, fortunately, I had studied a bit on my own during my painting, astronomy, and Carl Jung obsessions. She was a bit lonely in school, and when she moved to New York, I took her up to Claremont Riding Academy on the Upper West Side every week because the horses made sense to her, and for her. She moved back and forth between her dad's house in Nashville and mine in New York, and spent one year at a boarding school in Maryland where she could ride horses as part of the curriculum. She returned to New York to finish high school and graduated from Elizabeth Irwin, an old New York institution.

By tenth grade it was becoming apparent that Chelsea was a writer, but she decided to attend Memphis College of Art, where she studied photography and visual arts, and then settled permanently in the South again. She ultimately did become a writer, a cinematic songwriter who envisions and creates original sound-scapes, and has a hint of her grandfather's sense of rhythm, and a wildly creative prose writer, more so than I dreamed of being at her age. She released her first record in 2009, and has had to negotiate the rocky path of being an artist in her own way. When she finished writing the songs for her record, she called and asked the familiar question, "How do I have a successful career as a musician without having a public life? I don't *want* a public life." After thirty years of wrestling with that very conundrum, I still have no answer.

Chelsea has an independence of spirit that I recognize from my own life and my own impulses, but she has taken it a generational step further. I look up to Chelsea. She seems to have easily synthe-sized creative ideals that I spent my life struggling to even articu-late. And beyond the artistic, she and I are of like mind in many ways—the traditionally girlish topics of conversation and pursuits never interested either of us (or Caitlin, for that matter), and we each had to come to terms with being feminine women who lacked classically feminine interests, in absolute contrast to Hannah and Carrie, who are domestic goddesses to their very cores. That has changed somewhat for me as I've gotten older—I find all aspects of homemaking to be deeply relaxing and restorative, and they prob-ably will become so for Caitlin and Chelsea. (Even as I write this, Caitlin e-mails me from England to ask for recipes!)

I made my third album for Columbia, *Somewhere in the Stars*, late in 1981, when I was hugely pregnant with Chelsea, and we took a break before mixing it for me to give birth. When Chelsea was a few weeks old, I began taking her along with a load of baby gear into the studio to finish the record. I sat in the control room and put her in her baby chair on the other side of the glass in the studio, so I could sit at the console and watch her as she slept.

That album was not my best work. When we played it for the label heads of marketing and A&R, I could see that they were anxious and awkwardly trying to find something to say about the record, and ultimately trying to figure out what to do with it. Apart from not featuring any obvious country hits, it sounded disjointed and unfocused. I haven't listened to it in years, but my recollection is that I was distracted and self-conscious at the time, both in my life and in my work, and the music is an all too accurate reflection of that state of mind. I did go to Carmel to make a video with Michael Nesmith for one song, "I Wonder," which I performed on his television show, *Elephant Parts*. As everyone feared, *Somewhere in the Stars* didn't generate any big hits, and as a result I spent a good deal of time rethinking my whole approach to recording, and my career as a Nashville hitmaker, now without a hit, in general.

My next record did not, however, benefit from any of this reflection. After writing an entire album, I decided to try another producer, David Malloy, who had made a lot of hit records in Nashville. David and I got along very well and together made a big, flashy, in-your-face, somewhat edgy album. We hired Waddy Wachtel, Bob Glaub, and Vince Melamed, among others, to come from Los Angeles, and used the "Bette Davis Eyes" synthesizers and huge snare drum sounds that were so trendy in the mid-eighties. Columbia had assigned a new A&R guy to me, Eli Ball, and after listening to the record, he decided that it was not finished and insisted that I go back into the studio. (I shudder to think of how much money was spent on this project.) Eli and I did not make a good match; I found him abrasive and pushy, and I am certain that he found me intractable and reactionary. I decamped to New York, where Rodney came back into the picture. We hired drummer Anton Fig, bassist Willie Weeks, and Larry Crane, guitarist from John Mellencamp's band, to play on more sessions and started basic tracks again. Eventually we brought in a third producer, David Thoener.

Earlier in the recording process, I had received a call from Tom Petty's management asking me to come to Los Angeles and sing for a potential sound track, on a song called "Never Be You," which Tom had written with my friend Benmont Tench. The sessions were a little tough. Jimmy Iovine was producing, and I did not find him to be the most gracious person in the world. However, Hal Blaine was playing drums on the tracks, and again I was awestruck by him. Tom and Benmont were lovely, and I did my best, but I didn't feel I could deliver what Iovine wanted. Months later it became clear that "Never Be You" was not going to appear on the intended sound track, so I asked Tom and Benmont if I could record it myself, and they agreed. It was one of the new tracks we did in New York, along with a John Hiatt song, "Pink Bedroom." John was a favorite songwriter of mine, one to whom I felt genuinely connected and one of the few whose work I felt supremely confident in interpreting. The day we cut "Pink Bedroom" in New York was emblematic of the entire process of making the album: Larry Crane had an extremely aggressive acoustic guitar part to play on the song, and although he didn't complain about it, after a few hours of trying to get a basic track, he calmly pointed out that his fingers were bleeding. I was shocked and thoroughly unsettled by the literal blood on the tracks, but he and Rodney seemed to take it in stride, and we kept going. I can still see Larry wrapping his fingers between takes to stanch the blood, then taking a deep breath for the next take.

We did more recording in Los Angeles, and by January I was exhausted by the project. We had begun *Rhythm and Romance* on April 16, 1984, and we mastered it on April 15, 1985. At the end of that torturous year of recording, rerecording, mixing, and remixing in three cities, with three producers, one executive producer, and a lot of fighting, I found that I was suffering from a bizarre kind of trauma. I was absolutely determined that I would never set foot in a recording studio again. I hated the process, I hated the record, I hated Eli Ball, and I did not even want to think about promotion and touring for the record, which for me had become nothing but a painful memory.

The trauma continued even into the photography for the album cover. After a long day of shooting at a studio in Soho, I left at about ten that night with my arms full of clothes and got into a taxi with the stylist and the makeup artist. The taxi driver crossed himself when we got in, floored the gas pedal, got up some speed, and slammed right into a parked car, injuring the stylist, who had been sitting in the front. We all fell out onto the street, shaking, and got into another taxi, but that image of the driver crossing himself before he crashed, along with Larry's bleeding fingers, metaphorically summed up what that record meant in my life. I still cannot stand to listen to *Rhythm and Romance*, even though I think that some of its songs—"Second to No One" and "Halfway House" especially— are among my best to date. Perversely, the album quickly reached number one on the country charts, generating two number one and two top five singles. "I Don't Know Why You Don't Want Me," which I had written with Rodney, won a Grammy, my first, for Best Female Country Vocal Performance. (My mother, upon first hearing the song, had said that no country radio station would ever play it, as it was "too pop." I called her from the car as soon as I left the awards ceremony, Grammy in hand, and she made some quick revisionist, but apparently heartfelt, congratulations.) I also received the only award that has really meant anything to me, in retrospect, for that record: the prestigious Robert J. Burton songwriting award from BMI, my performing rights organization, for most-performed song of the year for "Hold On." At the time, however, I was still so un-settled and fragile from the months of work on *Rhythm and Ro-mance* that I went home the night I won the Burton award and pulled apart the lyrics of the song, going over them line by line with a deeply critical eye until I determined that it did not deserve the award in the least. Even though in my heart I could not really accept the accolade, it was encouraging, and gave me more confidence as a writer.

After a year or so, I received a letter from Columbia's lawyers in-forming me that I owed the label a record, and since I clearly was not in preproduction, I was in violation of my contract and they were suspending me. My contract would be extended by the amount of time I was in arrears. I got three or four more letters like this, but each time I crumpled them up and threw them away. Winning a Grammy had not done anything to change my mind about recording again. I toured a bit after *Rhythm and Romance*, but not seriously; my heart wasn't in any of it, even though I had the privilege of working with some of the most gifted musicians on the planet. Larrie Londin, one of the greatest drummers who ever lived, went on the road with me, and with Rodney as well, out of pure love for the music. Larrie was so much in demand as a session musician that he lost money by touring with us, but he did it anyway. He was such a dear soul. He was physically enormous, and he and I used to tease each other mercilessly. I told him fat jokes and called him names, and he told me my ass was just like Diana Ross's. (He should have known. He played behind both of us.) We adored each other. When we went out on the tour bus, I gave him the back bedroom, as he literally could not fit in one of the bunks. It was the least I could do. But even though I had wonderful opportunities to play live with people like Larrie for decent money, I didn't want to go out. I was enjoying summer afternoons at the house in Brentwood, taking care of the girls, playing volleyball with friends in the yard, having parties, and traveling for fun rather than work. My memories of *Rhythm and Romance* continued to distress me, and I still felt a deep exhaustion from the experience. The very thought of going back into the studio was overwhelming and enervating. After a year went by, Rodney started to talk to me about ideas for a new record, but I made it clear that I was not interested, and resisted every idea he had. He grew more insistent, but I remained unmoved.

During this time I got a call from my dad, in which he made some small talk and then said, "I have to ask you something. What's your royalty rate at Columbia?" I told him; he harrumphed, said, "Okay," and hung up. Shortly afterward, Columbia dropped him. I was devastated for him and, embarrassed that I was still on the label, started thinking about bigger changes for myself.

Months went by until one afternoon when I was sitting in the kitchen of the log house and Rodney rushed in through the back door, his eyes wide. "I have the vision for your record," he said excitedly. "I saw it all on the drive home from town." He described it— sonically, thematically, musically, and emotionally—in great detail, and the more he talked, the more I was drawn in, so contagious was his excitement. What he described that day was almost exactly what *King's Record Shop* turned out to be. He described a more roots-sounding record, not just in reaction to the heavy pop vibe of *Rhythm and Romance*, but as something fresh and more suited to my natural instincts. I studied Bob Dylan's *Writings and Drawings* as if it were the Dead Sea Scrolls, and dissected Guy Clark and Townes Van Zandt songs as exercises to better myself as a songwriter. I should, I thought, make a record that reflected *those* sensibilities. And most important, no big synthesizers and no executive producers.

We began recording on Valentine's Day of 1987, and the engineers had flowers waiting for me in the studio. I wore my black leather biker jacket to the first day of sessions, thinking that sartorial toughness would make me less nervous. But there was no need. There was genuine camaraderie in the studio and no drama or struggle. I felt like I was part of a working band again, a sentiment that had been entirely absent during the previous project. The studio was comfortable, the engineering crew was soothing and accommodating, and Rodney and I hit a stride musically.

During the weeks in the studio, the engineers pirated a pay-per-view channel that was showing *Aliens*, and we had the film running in a continuous loop on a monitor above the recording console. Throughout each day we would look up to watch a few minutes of the film, until we could all recite the dialogue in our sleep and knew every scene forward and backward. I still have a strange visceral connection between *King's Record Shop* and Sigourney Weaver and the terrifying creatures in that film. (Years later, the night of my first performance at Lincoln Center, my dear friend Liz Tirrell hosted a party for me after the show, which Sigourney attended. I told her about the bizarre association I had between her and the record, which seemed to amuse her.)

The musicians on the *King's* sessions were phenomenal. The great Barry Beckett was on keyboards, Michael Rhodes played bass, Eddie Bayers was on drums, and Rodney had found a tremendously gifted guitarist, Steuart Smith, whom I had met for the first time when we were in preproduction a few weeks earlier. I didn't understand Steuart's working style at first and made fun of him a bit to Rodney. He seemed extremely obsessive and overly meticulous, and I sensed a self-consciousness in his demeanor that made me feel awkward. I slowly realized, over the course of the first few weeks of work, that Steuart was one of the most deeply sensitive musicians I had ever encountered, and that the depths of his soul came right out the ends of his fingers when he played. Living in mundane reality was often almost excruciating for Steuart. He is not the first artist I have known with so few defenses against the world, and certainly there have been many, many times I have felt that vulnerable and exposed myself. He became a collaborator and such an inspiration to me that when I produced *Interiors* a few years later, I sought him out for help with arrangements, and he proved invaluable.

During the first week of working on *King's*, we recorded my dad's song "Tennessee Flat-Top Box." (I mistakenly thought it was in the public domain, its true author lost in the mists of time—an error that was made much of in the press later. Even my dad took out a full-page ad in the industry weeklies crowing about the fact that I hadn't known he had written it before I recorded it. He was delighted. In fact, it was a simple mistake: I had known my dad's version of the song for my entire life, the way that a child thinks that something she's been familiar with since birth must have always been there.) Eddie Bayers stopped after the first take, drumsticks in hand and tears in his eyes, and said to the rest of the band, "Pay attention, boys. We won't pass this way again." Randy Scruggs came in to play the signature guitar line, which was an emotional and musically satisfying experience for me, and the record became a huge hit.

A few years prior, when Albert Lee had left my touring band, Rodney suggested that I bring in this guy named Vince Gill to play lead guitar, and he went so far as to hire him before I had ever played with him or even met him. I showed up at rehearsal for a tour for *Rhythm and Romance* the first day with Vince in the band with a huge attitude against him. I was barely civil. I was distraught over losing Albert and I had no confidence that Vince, who came from the band Pure Prairie League, could fill Albert's shoes. During the very first song of the day, when it came to the guitar solo, Vince played a wicked, full-bore, wildly confident solo and I jerked my head around to look at him. I didn't say anything, thinking it might be a fluke. In the second song, he upped the ante when the instrumental break came and I was riveted, and stunned. An hour later, when we took a break, I gave it up to him right away. "I didn't think anyone could ever replace Albert," I said. "I apologize. You are incredible." He didn't say a word, just pushed the back door open and walked outside and yelled at the top of his lungs. The tension broke for both of us and we became great friends. (Vince, of course, was meant for much bigger things than being anyone's sideman.) He came in during *King's* to put on some background vocals. I had recently been invited to sing on a Yoko Ono tribute called *Every Man Has a Woman*, a record that had been John Lennon's idea. Yoko had asked me to sing a song called "No One Can See Me Like You Do," and Vince had performed gorgeous background vocals. (Going to Yoko's apartment in the Dakota to celebrate the release of the album was incredibly exciting for a diehard Beatles fan like myself. I had been so flustered when Rodney and I attended the party that I got out of the taxi and introduced myself to the doorman: "Hi, I'm Rodney Crowell, and this is Rosanne Cash." He just looked at me without smiling, as I'm sure I wasn't the first idiot to get dismantled by the proximity to John and Yoko.) I also recorded another John Hiatt song for *King's*, "The Way We Make a Broken Heart." It was a heady time for me, a pinnacle of success. But I wanted something else.

I t was late in the making of *King's* that I had a dream that changed my life.

I had met Linda Ronstadt a few times—in Los Angeles, while I was recording at Lania Lane; when I opened for Bonnie Raitt at the Greek Theater and Linda had come to see the show; and on a number of other occasions, as we traveled in the same circles and worked with many of the same musicians. Her record *Heart Like a Wheel* had profoundly affected me as a young girl, and I had studied it assiduously as a great example of a feminine point of view concept record, the best one since Joni Mitchell's *Blue*, I thought, and equally important in the template I was creating for what I might do in my life. I especially admired her thoughtful song selection, which resulted in a very well-balanced album, and I wanted to make a record with a similarly unified concept, but as a songwriter.

Just as I was beginning to record *King's*, I had read an interview with her in which she said that in committing to artistic growth, you had to "refine your skills to support your instincts." This made such a deep impression on me that I clipped the article to save it. A short time after that, I dreamed I was at a party, sitting on a sofa with Linda and an elderly man who was between us. His name, I somehow knew, was Art. He and Linda were talking animatedly, deeply engrossed in their conversation. I tried to enter the discussion and made a comment to the old man. He turned his head slowly from Linda to me and looked me up and down with obvious disdain and an undisguised lack of interest. "We don't respect dilettantes," he spat out, and turned back to Linda. I felt utterly humiliated and woke from this dream shaken to the core. I had been growing uneasy in my role in the Nashville community and the music business as a whole. I thought of myself primarily as a songwriter, but I had written only three songs on *King's*. I was famous and successful, but it felt hollow, and the falsehoods were piling up. With more success had come more pressure to be a certain way, to toe a certain line, to start a fan club (which I refused to do), to participate in big, splashy events, and to act as if the country music scene were a religion to which I belonged. I resisted the push to conform, to buy into a certain narrow aesthetic, and to become part of the established hierarchy. I didn't want a lofty perch; I wanted to be in the trenches, where the inspiration was. My unease led me to that dream. Carl Jung said that a person might have five "big" dreams in her life—dreams that provoke a shift in consciousness—and this was my first.

From that moment I changed the way I approached songwriting, I changed how I sang, I changed my work ethic, and I changed my life. The strong desire to become a better songwriter dovetailed perfectly with my budding friendship with John Stewart, who had written "Runaway Train" for *King's Record Shop*. John encouraged me to expand the subject matter in my songs, as well as my choice of language, and my mind. I played new songs for him and if he thought it was too "perfect," which was anathema to him, he would say, over and over, "but where's the MADNESS, Rose?" I started looking for the madness. I sought out Marge Rivingston in New York to work on my voice and I started training, as if I were a runner, in both technique and stamina. Oddly, it turned out that Marge also worked with Linda, which I didn't know when I sought her out. I started paying attention to everything, both in the studio and out. If I found myself drifting off into daydreams—an old, entrenched habit—I pulled myself awake and back into the present moment. I opened my eyes and focused. Instead of toying with ideas, I examined them, and I tested the authenticity of my instincts musically. I stretched my attention span consciously. I read books on writing by Natalie Goldberg and Carolyn Heilbrun and began to self-edit and refine more, and went deeper into every process involved with writing and musicianship. I realized I had earlier been working only within my known range—never pushing far outside the comfort zone to take any real risks. I had written songs almost exclusively about romance and all the attending little dramas of loss and lust. It was legitimate, certainly, but only one small mode of transportation over a vast landscape of experience that might be fodder for whole new catego-ries of songs. I started painting, so I could learn about the absence of words and sound, and why I needed them, and what I actually wanted to say with them. I took painting lessons from Sharon Orr, who had a series of classes at a studio called Art and Soul.

I remained completely humbled by the dream, and it stayed with me through every waking hour of finishing *King's Record Shop*. We were so far into the process that it was too late to add songs or change the ones that were there, but I vowed the next record would reflect my new commitment. Rodney was at the top of his game as a record producer, but I had come to feel curiously like a neophyte in the studio after the dream. Everything seemed new, frightening, and tremendously exciting. I had awakened from the morphine sleep of success into the life of an artist.

The cover of the *King's* album won a Grammy for best art direction. It was a photo of the actual King's Record Shop in Louisville, Kentucky, hand tinted by Hank DeVito. I had seen the image at Hank's house and begged him to retake the photograph with me standing in the doorway for my cover. He declined, as the hand tinting had been laborious, but he did agree to take my photo in a doorway and then digitally insert me into the original shot of King's Record Shop. I didn't actually visit the real store until the record was released, when we held a press conference there. Sadly, King's Record Shop has gone the way of most mom-and-pop record stores and no longer exists.

I ended up having four number one singles off *King's*, a first for a woman in the industry. Although it was my sixth album, I felt like a beginner, and I was relieved and grateful for the chance to start over, to go deeper into sound and texture, language and poetry, and the direction of my own instincts.

As I learned more about painting, I began to become obsessed with it. I was not a great visual artist by any stretch of the imagination, but I found a freedom in working with paint that I had never experienced as a musician. I grew curious to discover whether I could parlay the liberation I had felt on the canvas to the stage, from paint to my voice. I figured if I could experience it in one creative realm, I could find it in another. Painting so mesmerized me that I still remember going by myself one day to paint in one of the rooms in the warehouse where Sharon taught, working for hours and completely losing track of time. I became rattled when I discovered that it was nighttime and that I had been painting for five or six hours and was now alone in a warehouse in a dicey part of town. Attending a class with visual arts students was also a fresh way for me to cast off the trappings of fame, to unshackle myself from success and the expectations that went with it.

Not that I didn't take advantage of that success—I renegotiated my contract with Columbia, which by then was a part of Sony, after *King's Record Shop* and brazenly demanded an almost outrageous sum, but it seemed justified, as I not only had a lot of currency in the industry at that point, but I was angry about the fact that they had dropped my dad. I wanted parity from them, and at some level I didn't care if they renewed my contract or not—I simply wanted to paint. They gave me the amount I asked for. My longtime business manager, Gary Haber, had the good sense to put half of it in an IRA and pay some bills, and the rest of it saw me through the enormous difficulties that were to come. I never again achieved the kind of chart success I had with *King's*, and it took me years to recoup the advance that I had gotten from Sony. (In fact, when I left Sony in 1994, it was still unrecouped, and my new label, Capitol, had to take on my debt.)

As part of my attempt to unbind myself from language, I began listening obsessively to four records, all instrumentals: Miles Davis's *Kind of Blue* and *Sketches of Spain*; the sound track for the movie *Cal*, written by Mark Knopfler; and Peter Gabriel's sound track for Martin Scorsese's film *The Last Temptation of Christ*. When I needed a reprieve from the intensity of those four, I listened to Vaughan Williams. Slowly I began to write new songs, as an adjunct to my painting, and I started to get more involved in political and environmental issues. I also became pregnant again. I cherish one particular image of myself that sums up that period of my life: Seven and a half months' pregnant, and huge, I walked into a new painting class with a stack of voter registration cards and made an announcement that if anyone needed to register to vote, to see me. I can remember the shock on the students' faces. I eventually grew so enormous that Sharon, the teacher, got nervous that I was breathing in too much paint and might go into labor in class, and suggested that perhaps I should resume after giving birth.

Carrie Kathleen (named for my dad's mother, Carrie, and my sister Kathy) was born on December 12, 1988, almost two weeks overdue. She was a precious and welcome tonic in our lives at that moment, for we had moved from the log house into a big, featureless McMansion on Franklin Road in Nashville just a month before and were all feeling disoriented. Carrie was born only five months before Rodney's dad died and eighteen months before my marriage to Rodney would end, and it seemed that she came into the family to bind us in love, steel us against loss, and connect all the disparate personalities, come what may. My mother had come from California to Nashville in late November to be present at her birth, but I was so overdue that she had to return home before I went into labor. When she finally did meet baby Carrie for the first time a few months later, she looked at her and said with awe, "Rosanne, she's so special." She was indeed, and has grown even more so. Carrie was my foxhole partner through divorce, moving to New York, remarriage, September 11—and any number of other traumatic and revolutionary experiences. She attended Barrow Street Nursery School in New York when she and I lived in our little apartment on Morton Street in the Village, then went to St. Luke's on Hudson Street from pre-K through eighth grade, then to Rudolf Steiner High School on the Upper East Side for a year, and then she decided to finish her high school years with her dad in Nashville. Because she hates change and loves the safety of what she knows, that move represented a huge decision for her, one that required tremendous courage. I supported her in that decision, but God, I grieved when she left, fearing I would never have her in my house again. But true to her form, which is of deep family connection, community, and domesticity, after finishing high school and putting in one year of college in design school, she moved back home to New York and enrolled at the New School University and took a job at St. Luke's, her old alma mater, teaching a cooking class to young children after school. She has never caused me a single problem. John, my husband, who took on the role of a father to her when she was three, loves her deeply. She has matured into an exotic beauty, with her grandmother Vivian's Sicilian coloring and masses of black hair surrounding a heart-shaped face and feline eyes. She is quite heart-stopping, like a modern-day Claudia Cardinale, and remains dreamily unaware of the effect she has on men. John regularly gazes at her and sighs to me, "What do you think she's going to do with all that beauty?" Usually he adds wryly, "Shouldn't she marry a billionaire?" She is an odd little thing in many ways, highly sensitive to textures and colors and sounds, but she knows herself extraordinarily well, and she is proactive on her own behalf, always planning her life within the exact limits of her ability to navigate any given circumstance. She paints and draws, cooks and sews, and has dozens of skills and talents that I never dreamed of having. I thrill to her company, and just to the fact that she is in my life.

In 1989, when Carrie was about a year old, I had composed enough songs for a new album. (I was again on suspension from Columbia for being overdue in delivering a record.) The songs I had written were about the coming dissolution of my marriage—"postcards from the future," as I called them later—though I didn't realize it at the time. I didn't recognize the themes of heartbreak and disappointment and the obsession with hidden disillusionment running through every song, but it was definitely there, and everyone but me seemed to notice. Intuitively I knew Rodney shouldn't produce the record. He agreed, and I made appointments to meet with a few different producers I respected. I played Malcolm Burn the demos I had made of the new songs, and after listening quietly to all of them without commenting, he asked very directly when the tape ended, "And why aren't you producing this yourself?" I stuttered a couple of reasons that I realized made little sense, and then finally admitted, "I don't know." After he left, I paced the length of the room for about an hour, thinking about the possibility and eventually growing excited. I thought I could do it.

The label agreed, and I called Steuart Smith to work on some arrangements for me. Because he lived near Washington, D.C., we mailed demos back and forth in preparation for recording. I had the idea of approaching the record as if it were a collection of Celtic songs and decided to make it nearly all acoustic. Also, I didn't trust myself with drums—I was sick of the big snare sound of the eighties, and I didn't want to spend hours sorting out drum sounds, as had been my habit in the previous fifteen years of recording. Even after that revelatory session with Glyn Johns in 1980, it had never really occurred to me that I could record drums differently, without the hyperfocus on the exact snare and tom and kick effects, but a more stripped-down, percussive rather than full-kit sound was just right for this particular group of songs. I hired Roger Nichols to record and mix the record, and I booked a studio at Masterfonics in Nashville because it had a great old Trident recording console and I wanted to record in analog. Every studio in Nashville, and in the entire country for that matter, was in the process of switching to digital, and the Neve board/Studer tape machine combination that I had grown to think of as the gold standard in recording was going the way of Betamax. There were few analog boards left in town, and that old Trident seemed like a great option for me. (After I finished the record, I was crushed to learn that the board was sold to a jingles studio.)

I hung a sign above the door to the control room that read ABANDON THOUGHT, ALL YE WHO ENTER HERE. I was rebelling against overthinking, overproduction, and contrivances of any kind. I was determined to make this record as "organic" as possible—in concept, sonics, arrangement, choice of instruments, and recording technique. I didn't want to do a lot of preproduction, beyond the basic arrangements that Steuart had helped write. I hired Michael Rhodes and Eddie Bayers to join Steuart and me on the basic tracks, and the five of us, along with Roger, began recording. From the out-set it was an intensely satisfying experience. The gents did revolt at one point against my "no full drum kit" rule and insisted that I let Eddie play the full complement on a few songs. John Stewart, my dear friend and mentor, came in to record a guitar track on a song we had written together, "Dance with the Tiger," and my heart melted at the poignancy of his part. Mark O'Connor, Edgar Meyer, and other world-class musicians came in to play on several tracks, and I was in my element; I loved making this record as I had no other. The entire process was the antithesis of the *Rhythm and Romance* experience—civilized, measured, easy, and so musical.

When recording was complete, I went with Roger to Los Angeles to mix it, and my toddler Carrie and I settled into the Sunset Marquis. The mixing went especially well—Roger was such a strange and gifted person. I would begin to tell him something I wanted to try or something I wanted changed, and as soon as I opened my mouth, before I could say a word, his arm would be slowly reaching across the console to do the very thing I wanted. I remember that at one point during the recording, I had one request that couldn't be done—some technical thing that just couldn't be achieved on the Trident—and Roger spent a couple days inventing a device to over-ride the limitations of the analog board to get me what I wanted.

Steuart was, again, a gift, and I came to appreciate the full depth and breadth of his genius during *Interiors*. He and I started our own little autodidact club, making lists of books and talking about literature and philosophy over drinks. Even though Steuart and I parted musical ways many years ago (he has since become a member of the Eagles), to this day I have a very fond place in my heart for him and know that he fundamentally changed me as a musician, by inspiring me with the depth of his attention—to music, to books, and to life in general.

I took the finished record back to Nashville, totally proud of what I had accomplished, and played it for Rodney. "It's great," he said, "but I don't think it's finished." I was shocked. I remember lying on the floor next to the boom box that I had just used to play Rodney the tape, staring at the ceiling and wondering if he was right. He argued that the record was *too* interior, too quiet, with too much of the same monochromatic emotional and sonic palette, and suggested adding a few songs to balance it and give it more energy. I started to cry, but after thinking about it for a day, I reluctantly agreed that he should produce a few more songs for the record.

When Rodney hired Richard Bennett to play on my song "On the Inside," I started to feel that it might have been the right decision. I loved how Richard played and how "On the Inside" came out, and even thought it should open the record. There was another song, a ditty I had started and Rodney finished called "Real Woman," in which I had never had any faith, as I thought it was too self-conscious and not even a real song—I had begun writing it with tongue firmly in cheek, but Rodney took it seriously and finished the lyrics and suggested we record that as well. Even though I had reservations, I agreed. I was still so disconnected from "Real

Woman" that I left the studio after we got the basic track and let Rodney and Steuart work on the guitar parts. I came back at the end of the day to hear what they had done, and as I sat at the console a feeling of dread flooded through me. "What do you think?" Rodney asked. "I think it sounds like a fucking Pepsi commercial," I said, and left the studio, almost distraught. I thought that song had ruined the record. Rodney and Steuart were shocked. Although Rodney rethought it a bit so that it didn't turn out too badly, I still have not listened to that track in nearly twenty years.

"Real Woman" is probably my greatest musical regret—even more than the giant snare/synthesizer sounds of the mid-eighties, or some of the more sophomoric, navel-gazing songs I wrote for *Rhythm and Romance*. To my mind, it completely diluted the artistry of the record, and the only thing that could salvage it even today would be a great R&B singer like Anita Baker taking it to a whole other level of empowerment.

I delivered *Interiors* to the label, and they sent the head of A&R to the studio to listen to a few key tracks with me. After listening to four songs, he laughed coldly and said, "We can't do anything with that." He looked at me with bemusement. He was clearly flabbergasted that I thought this was music the label would consider commercially viable. I was stunned, and felt as if I had been slapped in the face. He explained further: "Radio won't play this." When he left the studio, I started to get angry. To my mind this was the most "country" record I had given them—almost entirely acoustic, very folk based, a real singer-songwriter project. I said to the assistant engineer, who was with me in the control room, "He's wrong. I can't wait to prove him wrong." He was, as it happened, right. The first single, "What We Really Want," made it only to number 39, my weakest showing on the country charts in well over a decade. My heart sank, and I started to become nervous about the album's prospects. After that, nothing happened; the label abandoned the project. About three months after *Interiors* came out, I was on a plane staring out the window and thinking about what I should do. I knew the life of that record was effectively over—Columbia would not put any money or effort into another single, and yet . . . it was the most heartfelt, most artful thing I had ever done in my life.

I suddenly realized that I could no longer work with Columbia Nashville, and after talking to Rodney, my dad, and my manager at the time, Will Botwin, I decided to ask the label to transfer me to the New York division. (Dad had given me the best, and most succinct, advice, born of years of arguing, wrangling, convincing, and coaxing music industry executives to understand or support him: "Screw 'em," were his exact words. "You belong in New York.") Will offered to go into the meeting with me, but I told him I wanted to do it alone. I met with Roy Wunsch, then the head of the label in Nashville, and a few other key people. I told them that I was well aware that the record hadn't performed for them, and warned them, kindly, that this situation was going to get worse, because this was what I was going to do from now on. I said that we would likely both be unhappy in the future, so I felt it was in their best interests to transfer me. The gentlemen seemed relieved. Roy shook my hand and said, "We'll miss you," and that was it. I walked out into the hall, the door closed behind me, and I actually had to lean against the wall, I was so dizzy. Twelve years on this division of the label, and it was over in twenty minutes. That transfer on paper to New York in 1990 was the beginning of my transfer of body and soul to New York completely. I had just met John Leventhal, and I knew my life was going to change, although I couldn't foresee how profound and how permanent the change would be.

With my transfer at the label, the end of my marriage, and my departure from Nashville, I entered a storm of a magnitude I could scarcely have imagined. With the press—and many of my friends—excoriating me for all those decisions, I moved with all the girls to Westport, Connecticut, for the summer of 1991, even though I was touring during almost that entire period, and then to Manhattan in the first week of September 1991. The older girls returned to Nashville and their schools there, and only Carrie remained with me when I rented my first apartment in the Village, paying for an entire year in advance. At 13 Morton Street we soon befriended Velvet Abashian, who had a tiny real estate office on the ground floor of our building. Actually, Velvet befriended us, for every time she saw me coming up the stoop with Carrie in the stroller, she came out and lifted both in through the front door. Her kindness made her a dependable ally as I negotiated living in New York with a toddler on my own. I enrolled Carrie at Barrow Street Nursery School and did a lot of traveling back and forth to Nashville to see her sisters while I tried to figure out how to uproot their lives and bring them to live with me.

During this period I did my best to keep my head down, refusing to respond to the accusations and rumors that had been circulating in the press or among my friends—that I had become a lesbian, that I was having an affair with Will Botwin, that I had bleached my hair blond and was taking drugs—or to the "interviews" that I had supposedly given, in which I deplored Rodney and my former life. None of it was true, but all of it was too tawdry to warrant a response, I thought. In the midst of all this, *Interiors* was receiving rapturous critical reception and was nominated for a Grammy in the category of Best Contemporary Folk Recording. I felt vindicated, and thrilled. I had toured fairly extensively in back of the record, with just Steuart and bassist Jim Hanson, and the experience had refined me as a musician in so many ways—I had to play a lot more guitar than I had been accustomed to, and I had to carry a show that was composed of rather dark material but make it seem elegiac. I did a pretty good job. John Leventhal even came to see me when I played Town Hall in New York, visiting backstage to say that he loved the show. (I know now what a rare occurrence it is to impress John.) John Prine wound up winning the Grammy for *The Missing Years*, and I was genuinely happy for him—John was an old friend, and certainly deserved the honor. I had gotten the validation I wanted for *Interiors*, and I was ready to move on.

I decided to ask John Leventhal to produce my next record, describing to him the songs I was writing as "elemental." I told him that my new song "The Wheel" would be the central piece of the record—he had heard me perform it live—and I also wanted it to be the title of the album. The recurring themes, I explained, were of fire and water, wind and moon, and I wanted the sonics to somehow reflect the references to the elements. I don't think he really understood me, and it's true that at the time I was deep in some foggy quasi–New Age mind-set in a weak attempt to detach from the tremendous pain I was actually in over the divorce and the effect it was having on my children. I was ungrounded and spinning from all the changes in my life. He agreed to produce the record but said he wouldn't do it alone, arguing that since *Interiors* I should think of myself as a producer as well, so he would coproduce it with me, with equal billing.

Before we started *The Wheel*, I asked him to produce a single track of my song "From the Ashes" for a charity compilation album, and we went into Electric Lady Studio on Eighth Street in New York to do it. I have a searing image from that session, one that marked a before-and-after moment in my life. I was sitting at the console, and John was standing next to me with his yellow Telecaster strapped across his body. He was about to do a guitar overdub while plugged directly into the board. When he started playing, everything fell away from him: self-consciousness, a desire to please, distraction, tension, fatigue, and even ideas about what he would play. He was absolutely, profoundly in the moment. I was seduced, heart, mind, and body.

We fell in love while we were making *The Wheel*. When we started the record, we were crazy with longing for each other but remained reserved, as we were both still extricating ourselves from our previous relationships. By the end of the record, we were a couple.

By then I had moved from Morton Street to a loft on Mercer Street in Soho, and John was spending most of his time there.

Chelsea moved to New York, and I enrolled her at St. Luke's

with Carrie. The following year Caitlin moved up, and we moved to a bigger place, occupying the top three floors of a brownstone at 241 West Eleventh Street in the Village. We settled into a life together there, and all three girls went to St. Luke's, just a few blocks away. By this time, Hannah was graduating from high school in Nashville. That was a good year for me, with all three girls in the same school, in the tight community and protection of St. Luke's. I loved the school, and I loved the girls being there. And yet, with John and me in the second year of our relationship, it became a little rocky as John suddenly found himself a father to three girls, two of whom were adolescents and resentful of the fact that I had pulled their lives apart. Much of the time, our desire to make it work outweighed our skills in managing the difficulties, but desire can become commitment, and commitment can make the forces of the universe work to your advantage. That's what happened for us.

*The Wheel* was a satisfying and truthful record, and conveyed— for me anyway—the crazy longing and lust of new love. (Years later I met John Hockenberry and his wife, Alison, at a party, and they told me how they had fallen in love listening to *The Wheel* while working as journalists in Afghanistan, interviewing people who later became al-Qaeda. That was one of the most strange and gratifying stories I heard about how the record affected other people.) I still have a lot of affection for it. It wasn't commercially successful, however, and I had to start thinking seriously about what I wanted to do with my life and how I could reinvent a forum for my work that was outside Top 40 radio, since that avenue was closing for artists like me. Will Botwin, who had been my manager for a decade by this time, had left management for a job at Columbia. He introduced me to Danny Kahn, who has been my manager since. I had heard around that time that Columbia was going to focus more energy and put more marketing dollars behind two of my contemporaries and labelmates, Shawn Colvin (with whom John had worked for many years and had been romantically involved) and Mary Chapin Carpenter. We had appeared together as a trio at "Bobfest," the huge extravaganza held at Madison Square Garden to celebrate Bob Dylan's thirtieth anniversary in music. I became nervous; I had been on the label a long time, longer than either of them, and felt I might be taken for granted at this point. I knew I had to do something proactive on behalf of my own future interests.

I went in, alone again, to see Don Ienner, the head of Columbia.

"I'm about to turn forty," I told him, "and I have to make some changes in my life. I know my contract isn't up, but I'm asking you to release me from it so I can find out what I want to do.

"This is about a life change," I explained, "not a label change. Please."

He looked surprised and then became pensive. "This is painful," he finally said. "I respect your decision, but I will genuinely miss you."

"Thank you, Donnie," I said, and I knew his sentiments were sincere. "I'll never say a bad word about you."

He smiled. "I didn't think you would."

*The Wheel* might have been over from a marketing standpoint, but it did find its audience. Even today, if I do a show and don't sing "The Wheel," it is guaranteed that someone will find me, write me,

or send a note backstage expressing disappointment and indigna-
tion that I neglected to perform the "most important song" in my
repertoire. And repertoire is destiny. I'm still crazy in love with John
Leventhal.


John and I were married on April 30, 1995, in a sculpture garden on
Elizabeth Street on the Lower East Side of Manhattan. Actually, it
was more a sculpture *lot* than a garden, as the statues, which were
scattered around on an area of gravel surrounded by a chain-link
fence, were all for sale. Still, it made for a beautiful setting, and em-
bellished with a tent, huge floral arrangements, and a faux bridge
leading from the street, it wound up looking like a comfortably
shabby urban version of the Borghese Gardens. At around four fifteen in the afternoon I stepped out of a town car with my mom at
the rear entrance to the garden and immediately saw John standing
twenty feet from me, his back turned, his black hair spilling over the
back of his collar. His shoulders filled out his dark suit tensely as he
stood looking toward the tent where we would shortly take our
vows. He was holding a blue umbrella, as it had started to drizzle
and was quite chilly. My dad came up to my mother and me and
began to tell us something, but I was mesmerized by John's back, by
his silhouette against the gray mist, and by the blue umbrella, so I
didn't hear what he was saying. Dad looked at me questioningly and
softly called my name, and I startled. "I just realized that he's my
husband," I explained, dazed. "It's something about the umbrella."

· · · · ·

My parents were both Southerners, but their respective Souths were worlds apart.

My father was from the Mississippi Delta, the bottomland, where families struggled for their lives and livelihoods, and were constantly at the mercy of storms and floods and droughts—which had a profound impact on their view of the world and their place in it. My mother grew up middle class, in San Antonio, Texas. She was the daughter of Tom and Irene Liberto, staunch, devout Catholics and second-generation Italian Americans. (In the immigrant exhibit at the Institute of Texan Cultures in San Antonio, there hangs an enormous portrait of my great-grandparents, Angelina and Frank Liberto, who came from Sicily in the late nineteenth century.) Tom Liberto, my grandfather, was a bespectacled insurance salesman who was also an amateur magician, champion gin rummy player, and rose gardener and breeder so renowned that he was asked to create a special rose for Lady Bird Johnson on her visit to San Antonio in the early 1960s. The Lady Bird Johnson rose was never produced commercially, but my grandfather was enormously proud of having been chosen for the assignment. My grandmother Irene Liberto came from a long line of elegant, feisty women who stayed home, but also stayed fully *themselves*.

Irene and Tom had a solid marriage and three children: my uncle Ray (the aforementioned honky-tonk piano player), my mother, Vivian, and my aunt Sylvia, who would talk to me about sex and any number of adult topics that my mother, somewhat of a prude, was too shy or mortified to address. Grandma Irene was a funny, lovely woman who was also an alcoholic. Many times my mother would come home from school and find my grandmother passed out on the sofa. My mother would frantically clean the house and get the dinner going before my grandfather got home so he would not be aware of his wife's condition. My grandfather—who was probably also an alcoholic but not the "designated patient," like my grandmother—was a taskmaster and had very rigid ideas about family life and gender roles, and operated from a narrow moral certitude. This had a profound effect on my mother, who lived with a lot of shame and a sense of heavy secrecy. She did, however, keep an impeccably clean house, as she had an absolute terror of dirt and untidiness.

Irene's sister, Mamie, was gorgeous in her youth, with a figure that made young men swoon. She retained her full breasts, long, shapely legs, and trim waist well into her seventies. She was also so deeply attached to her mother, whom we always called Nanny, that when she grew up and married, she moved across the street from Nanny so they could "visit" every day over coffee. (Nanny, who lived to be over a hundred, had extraordinary skin, remaining virtually unwrinkled into her nineties. In fact, all the Liberto women, most especially my mother, had gorgeous, flawless skin and aged beautifully.) Aunt Mamie was married to Uncle Bud, and they appeared to me to have a much more fluid, fun relationship than my grandparents. They were deeply, extravagantly in love for over sixty years. They called each other "sweetheart" and "precious" and "angel" throughout their lives, and I remember Aunt Mamie stroking Uncle Bud's hair as she stood in back of his easy chair, asking, "Can I get anything for you, darling?" When she died, Uncle Bud was inconsolable. He cried and visited her grave every day, until he just surrendered to his grief and died a few years later.

Their grand love story was matched only by that of Aunt Louise and Uncle Joe, relatives on my dad's side. Louise, Dad's oldest sister, and Joe lived across the road from each other in Dyess, Arkansas, and fell in love in their youth. Although they planned to marry, Uncle Joe first decided to see the world, joining the navy in 1940 and shipping off to the South Pacific. Uncle Joe's ship, the USS *Houston*, was sunk on March 1, 1942, which happened to be Aunt Louise's birthday. Uncle Joe was taken prisoner by the Japanese, and after a few years he was presumed dead. Aunt Louise grieved deeply, but recovered, married, and had a son, Damon. After nearly four and a half years of unspeakable torture, deprivation, illness, and loneliness, Uncle Joe, to the utter shock of everyone, returned home, malnourished and sick but alive. Aunt Louise extricated herself from her marriage, and she and Joe married in 1946. They had three children and lived together in marital bliss for fifty-seven years, until Aunt Louise died in April 2003.

Uncle Joe was the gentlest and kindest person I've ever met. He never uttered a bad word about a single soul, not even to condemn his captors—he rarely spoke about his suffering in the POW camp. He always had a smile on his face and never complained. Aunt Louise died shortly after Uncle Joe received the Purple Heart, sixty-one years after the USS *Houston* was sunk. He was presented with the award by my cousin Roy Cash, Jr., who at the time was a commander in the navy, inspired to military service by Uncle Joe, and who had most famously cowritten my dad's 1958 classic "I Still Miss Someone."

Uncle Joe and Aunt Louise, Aunt Mamie and Uncle Bud—those were the marriages I held up as a template for my own. "Can I get anything for you, darling?" is a mandate for me in the civilized conduct of an active marriage of minds and hearts—not servility, but charming, even effusive solicitude.

My parents might have achieved that kind of love story, and in the early days of their relationship, they did. There was no recovering their dreams of everlasting love once the endless touring and the amphetamines took hold of my dad's life, and the anguish and bitterness took hold of my mom's—even if their marriage might have recovered from it somewhat, they had probably shared too much acrimony during that period for it to be ultimately possible. The emotional debris field between them after thirteen years was enormous, too immense for them to cross toward each other, and by then June was there on Dad's side, waiting to be his wife, something they both felt was destined, given how, my father's story went, he told her he was going to marry her upon their first meeting backstage at the Grand Ole Opry, when he was still very much married to my mother.

To counter the enormous strain of their breakup on us children, I developed a philosophical perspective on my parents' marriage. I remember sitting in my grandmother Carrie's house soon after my mother had filed for divorce. After showing me a newspaper article that reported my mother had filed on grounds of "extreme cruelty" on the part of my father, my grandmother remarked, with so much sadness in her voice, "Honey, your daddy is *not* cruel." I knew that. I knew all his impulses of violence and destruction were self-directed. Oddly, my mother was the one who was much more demonstrative with her pain and anger, and the detritus of that fell on me and my sisters. Their marriage couldn't have lasted, and that did indeed break my mother's heart, a heartbreak that was complicated by her Catholicism, which in the mid-sixties was inflexible and unforgiving toward divorce. Understandably, she was unable to see the bigger picture, which is that Dad was meant to end up with June. My parents had a classic youngsters' marriage, one in which each party is blind to his or her own deep character flaws and can see them only in the reflection of the spouse. When too much childhood damage is there—and both of my parents were deeply damaged—then the flaws take on enormous weight and proportion. They could not escape themselves in the eyes—or the heart—of the other.

Dad and June by no means had a perfect marriage, but they understood each other and they shared music and fame together, as well as a deep love and fundamental respect. There were a lot of drug addicts in the extended family who caused tremendous strain in their marriage—not to mention Dad's almost constant struggle with his own addiction to painkillers and psychotropic drugs and June's later use of narcotics. They endured through their devotion in a kind of shared foxhole mentality. If notoriety was like an empire they were compelled to tend, they were also each other's refuge.

Within a few days after the divorce was final, my mother remarried, to Dick Distin, a former police officer in Ventura County, and she settled into a life that was really perfect for her—one filled with friends, parties, clubs, lessons, gardening, and church. She did needlework and she danced and bowled and painted and cultivated a wide circle of close relationships. She was active in her church and her community and became somewhat of a star in her little town.

My dad, of course, belonged to the world and had for quite some time. It was excruciating for her to turn on the television and see my dad and June together, talking about their great love and their musical connections. To her credit, however, she never said an ill word about Dad to us children. She restrained herself admirably in commenting about June as well, considering the depth of her resentment, but there were times she tossed off a venomous indictment and I could see the vast well of pain and bitterness she carried. She carried it for the rest of her life.

My dad did not just happily move on. He became much quieter and more reflective during the dissolution of their marriage, particularly once he was off the amphetamines and barbiturates and was thinking clearly. Many years later, when I was in my thirties, he told me that, after the formal split from my mother, when he'd first left Southern California and taken occupancy of his house on the lake in Tennessee, he'd walked the ground floor of the vast house, still nearly empty of furniture, late into the night. One time, he said, he'd walked from one end to the other, from the round room that overlooked the lake to the round room at the other end that was fitted into the side of the hill, feeling he was searching for something. *What's missing? Where is it?* he kept thinking. Suddenly he stopped in the middle room of the long floor and cried out my name at the top of his lungs. That was a powerful image for me, because at the time of his departure, in my twelve-year-old mind, I thought it had been easy for him to leave, and that he had not looked back.

Over thirty-five years later, a few weeks after his death in 2003, when the house had been emptied of decades of collected furniture and dishes and paintings and instruments, some sent off to each of us children and the rest dispatched to Sotheby's for sale, I walked alone on the ground floor, from round room to round room, and when I was sure that the lawyers and my siblings were busy on the upper floors and could not hear me, I stood in the middle room of the long floor and called out his name. It felt good to answer him, the echo of his voice reaching me so many years later, the echo of mine going back to the past and ending in that moment. It seemed that he heard me, and we both acknowledged the losses.


I had never been a girl who fantasized about weddings or having babies. Having come of age in the sixties, I thought there was something regressive, and repressive, about the whole idea, and my friends and I were all convinced that after high school we would just stop shaving our legs and move to a commune in Santa Barbara. I wanted to be a writer, and I wanted to do something transcendent and special with my life. The idea of settling down to the laundry every day and having children and getting together with other bored mothers for recreational activities truly terrified me. I remember a dream I had at age thirteen in which I was playing cards with my mother and grandmother in a small house. I was old and aware that my life was nearly over—a realization that left me desperate with regret. When I woke from that dream, I made a vow to myself, as serious as any vow I would make as an adult, that I would not permit myself to lead an unconscious existence, that I would not become complacent, that I would not allow my life to be defined by the petty and mundane. Even at that early age, I recognized that the card games in my dream represented some form of intellectual atrophy. (In my current life, I have enjoyed plenty of games of poker on the road with the guys in the band without seeming to court imminent spiritual disaster, and sometimes doing laundry is as calming as a Zen meditation. Flexibility is as essential as principle.) It was music that kept the passion for transcendence alive in me in the succeeding years.

Even when I was only ten years old, though my friends and I all worshipped the Beatles, I was conscious of feeling something more powerful and more adult about the band—a territoriality and identification that didn't make sense. I couldn't articulate those feelings to anyone, but I knew that they represented the kind of inner life I wanted—the songwriting, the liberation, the backbeat. My mother must have sensed this fervor in me, and even respected it, however little she might have comprehended it. The night the Beatles first appeared on *The Ed Sullivan Show*, my mother kept my sisters out of the living room, where I was glued to the television. She shushed them, saying, "Rosanne's watching the *Beatles*." My dad did understand the appeal and the kind of energy they aroused in me, on a lot of levels, and brought autographs of all four Beatles home to all four of his daughters. I still have mine.

If my commitment to a higher ideal kept me from fantasizing about marriage, it did not preclude fantasies about love. I found it first with Rodney. Marriage started to seem a natural stage in the progression of a romance, and besides that, my parents were eager for me to make our cohabitation legal. We married in 1979, when I was twenty-three years old, and I effectively ended my childhood with him. We were not only perfectly suited to help each other resolve the most egregious character traits left from our difficult childhoods, but we bonded in exhilarating creative and philosophical exploration. Unfortunately, we were both fairly untethered to anything earthbound and, finally, were too similar. While we ruminated dreamily on philosophy and music and metaphysics and art, neither of us knew where to find a post office, or how to change the oil in the car, or whether we even owned a key to the front door of the house. Ultimately, we both had to belatedly grow up, and we recognized that we couldn't do it together. We had four daughters, and it was excruciating for them, and for us, to split, but today each of the girls has told me on separate occasions, "I can't believe you and Dad were ever married. You're so unsuited to each other!"

I grew up, and into John. We were "in each other all along," as Rumi says, but we both had to develop to a point where we could fit each other's lives. He pulled me back down onto the planet, into the world, and into my own body. He was a pragmatist, a truth-teller, and one of the most extraordinarily gifted musicians I had ever known, a native New Yorker with a deep love and vast knowledge of roots and Southern music—and he was incredibly funny. That combination was irresistible to me. I had little pragmatism and a lot of magical thinking. My sense of truth had always been distorted by my idiosyncratic upbringing and by the secrets that were inherent in my father's drug addiction and how that had played out in our family life. An astrologer friend of mine looked at my and John's charts shortly after we got together and concluded with a sigh, "The two of you would make one *great* person." That assessment used to rankle both of us, as if we had to fill in the other's blanks, but now I see that relationship as the ultimate in companionship. We revel in the other's differences now. He is endlessly fascinating to me; unknowable and thrilling, and familiar and safe. I'm always excited to see him at the end of a day.

We were married by Rabbi Joseph Gelberman, somewhat of a star in mystical Judaism in New York. He showed up only minutes before the ceremony was to take place, leaving John about to come out of his skin with anxiety that he wouldn't actually appear. As a result, the ceremony started in a slightly unsettled state for everyone but the unruffled rabbi. In our meeting with him a few months earlier, John had made it clear that he did not want to speak Hebrew during the wedding since he had never been bar mitzvahed; his mother was Catholic and his father Jewish, but he had not been raised with any religion. The rabbi had agreed, but during the wedding he slipped into Hebrew and calmly instructed John, "Repeat after me." For the first and only time in his life, John found himself speaking in Hebrew, and even smashed the glass at the conclusion of the ceremony. My father, who also gave a reading, may have been more thrilled than anyone present that day. When I had told him that John and I were getting married, he said with a sigh of pleasure, "Thank God. I've been waiting forty years for one of my daughters to marry a Jew." Shortly afterward, he wrote John an awkward but loving letter, expressing his satisfaction that "a Jew was finally being brought into his bloodline."

After the ceremony, the entire party walked a few blocks to the Puck Building on Lafayette Street for our wedding reception. While I was on the dance floor, my dad came up to me at the end of a song and pulled me aside. Staring at me intently with a mixture of shock and hope, he said, "You're pregnant!"

"No, Dad," I answered, laughing. "But . . . as soon as possible!"

Dad and June went to London to do some shows a day or so later, and John and I headed to Rome for our honeymoon around the same time. On the morning we arrived, we were sitting in the roof-top café of our hotel at the top of the Spanish Steps, having a coffee and reading the international papers, when I saw an item in the *Herald Tribune* reporting that Dad had had some kind of attack on the flight to London and, upon arriving at Heathrow, had immediately gotten back on a plane and returned to the States. Sighing, I threw down the paper, knowing full well that he hadn't had any sort of "attack." He had left the wedding reception early, and I was aware that he had been taking a lot of pills recently because of excruciating pain from his jaw, which had been broken by a dentist while trying to remove a cyst years earlier and had been causing him intolerable pain since. I had convinced myself that his drug use was under control, and I felt betrayed again by my assumption that Dad was more or less straight, only to discover how seriously out of it he had become. I had spent virtually my entire life in denial about the depth of addiction in so many people I love—Dad being the first, the imprimatur of my denial. It had caused me a lot of anguish, and my default position had always been to interpret the pain as betrayal. I later came to learn that a drug addict betrays no one but himself, and I didn't have to become an accomplice in anyone's personal dramas. But at that moment, in early May of 1995, on my honeymoon, I could only feel hurt. I put down the paper and put my feelings about the incident completely aside and turned my attention to the contours of my new life with John. The next day we traveled from Rome to the Amalfi Coast.

As it turned out, Dad was off by only a week or so in his guess about my pregnancy. I conceived in Ravello that week, but I lost the baby seventeen weeks later, in late August. John was remarkably gentle and solicitous of my feelings and health, but I knew he was in a significant amount of pain himself. I wanted to turn to my parents for comfort. My mother tended not to be at her best in these situations, as her natural impulse was to withdraw into her own grief, metabolizing the suffering of her children as if it were her own. Dad was much better in dealing with raw grief, having experienced so much himself, and did not possess any inherent need to fix other people or solve their problems. I howled into the phone when I told him of our loss. He listened quietly, only murmuring little grunts of sadness. When I finished, he told me a story about his own mother, kneeling in the fields after the death of Jack, his brother, and how she thought she couldn't make it through another moment. She would cry out to God to help her, and then that moment was accomplished, and soon another day had passed. And then another. Then he gave me some advice, something he seldom did unless it was specifically solicited. "Cling to John," he said. "I've seen so many couples break up because of the loss of a child." I took that advice seriously, and it was the clinging to each other that got John and me through that time, and strengthened us, when so much potential for disintegration afflicted us. Later, when we faced other hard times, we had that first, devastating loss to remind us that we could stay together through just about anything. It was so typical of Dad that no matter how strung out he was, if the occasion demanded it, he could reach inside himself to that inextinguishable wisdom and intuition and offer something from it to soothe or enlighten.

Shortly after our conversation he also wrote me this letter:

Aug. 28 '95

Bon Aqua TN

Dear Rosanne

I was driving down to the farm this afternoon, grieving for you, when suddenly I felt the presence of my mother so strong that it was overwhelming.

I clearly saw her death again, but it wasn't painful this time.

In my mind's eye I saw several angels come down to each side of her, bear her spirit up and away and out of sight. It was a scene of total silence yet great joy. As I had seen at her death, again there was an "attitude" in the air, saying, "we are simply going about our unearthly business."

I'm not trying to get dramatic or otherworldly, Rosanne. This is what I saw and felt.

I slowed down to a crawl in the right lane of the interstate, because, feeling mama's presence and the angels so strongly, I shouted aloud, "Don't go away!" And, thinking of how the angels had ministered spiritual things to my mother as she was dying, I said, "Go to Rosanne and minister to her because she desperately needs you. In the name of the Lord I ask this."

So baby, this afternoon I sent my mother's friends to you. I'm sure that her spirit brought this about. She loved/loves you so much. And tonight I entreat the holy angels, your grandmother's friends to stay with you and help bring about your (and John's) healing. The scars will be deep, but there is power in the spirit here.

You must start to gain strength now and somehow rise above the pain of all this. Your family loves you very much, and although the days and nights will be hard for a while you will persevere.

> All my love
> Dad

I signed a new recording contract with Capitol Records, and in the months after the loss of our baby, John and I made a record together called *10 Song Demo*, which became an essential way for me to work out my grief. I can't hear any of that record now without recalling the sadness of that time, and the quiet days spent in John's basement studio on East Twelfth Street, recording those songs with sparse arrangement and heavy hearts.

One day in 1988, I was lying on my couch, in a sleepy reverie as the afternoon sun spilled through the huge bay window in the living room of my log house outside Nashville, when it occurred to me, in a sharp, unsettling way, that—

I was a singer. Not only was I a singer, but I sang for a living, which meant that a lot of people who were strangers to me were familiar with my voice without knowing me personally. They might not even know my name, but they had heard and now could recognize the Voice, a product of my genes and experience: authentic, but extremely personal, in my estimation.

This was largely how I felt about my voice—that it was undependable, beyond my control, somewhat embarrassing at times; if not too low, then too high; if not too soft, then too loud, or too harsh, or too wimpy. It was simply not enough, not right, and as such it exposed me far, far more than I could comfortably allow. It presented the perfect conundrum, and therefore an irresistible career choice.

My ambivalent relationship with my voice certainly had something to do with the fact that, thanks to my father's profession, our family was exposed to great singers—great singers who were also extraordinary personalities—from an early age. My mother, for her part, was a devoted Patsy Cline fan, and would say her name with slightly pursed lips: "Patsy . . ."—no last name needed, vowels squeezed a little by disapproval, but the tight mouth holding back a barely contained thrill. Patsy was wicked and fabulous when both qualities really meant something, before they became cheap ideas used to market more marginal talents. She was the object of fascination, distrust, and raw, if hidden, admiration. But not judgment: There was nothing to attach judgment to because Patsy did not judge herself. She was too truly and spontaneously alive, too rooted in her body, too in command of a startling sexuality that infused everything and that was the vehicle for a preternaturally affecting voice that both revealed and obscured her essence.

People who have genuine memories of her have become somewhat revisionist in their collective retelling. She was so great (also in the premarketing sense of the word) that they have felt almost obliged to polish and repair her wild and willful personality to suit the magnitude of her talent, particularly since she was a woman in an era that did not suffer female unaccountability gladly.

I once asked Mom what she remembered about Patsy—not as someone who would have a professional take (for that I would have called my dad), but as a woman who had been so deeply affected by her. She laughed but didn't ask why I had posed the question. "I didn't know her well," she admitted, "but your daddy and I did have her over to the house not long before she died. She had a mouth like a sailor, and she didn't put on airs. She was just Patsy, comfortable in her skin. I admired that. But that beautiful voice and body were so different from her . . . roughness." Mom paused. "I love her singing," she said passionately, present tense, and after considering the matter a while added, "Well, she was very *friendly*."

I laughed, my revisionist theory confirmed. "Were you disillusioned when you met her, Mom?"

"Well, I wouldn't want that to be said. She was ahead of her time, that's all." There was a quiet pause, then a little sigh. "I never got pictures with her."

Patsy Cline's gifts were extraordinary enough to have become a profound source of inspiration even to those of us without immediate memories of her, those of us whose voices weren't so full-bodied and fully formed from the beginning and whose values were not so exquisitely self-determined. In my private quandaries about my own voice, it gave me a lot of satisfaction to connect her teeming personality to the gifts she possessed. She lived a life utterly her own, messy and self-defined, and it all fed and merged with that voice.

At the end of our conversation, I couldn't help asking, "Mom, was I at that party?"

"Sure, honey! That was in, let's see, 1963? All you kids were born then."

I sighed wistfully. Somewhere in the blackout of early childhood I had had an encounter with Patsy Cline. I may spend the rest of my life trying to remember it.

(When I recorded "She's Got You," a song Patsy had made famous, for my record *The List* in 2009, I was nearly paralyzed with intimidation. I could not get *her* voice out of my head in order to sing the song myself. I finally thought to just ask for her permission, if she didn't mind, and I felt the pressure lift. The rest of the session went smoothly.)

The other great touchstone was, of course, Tammy. I first saw her in person in the early seventies at one of my father's "guitar pulls," at which a lot of musicians and songwriters would gather in his living room to preview their new work. I was about nineteen years old at the time, with teenage insouciance to spare, and the honored guests were George Jones and Tammy Wynette. I sat slack-jawed and transfixed as they sang "(We're Not) The Jet Set," with Tammy perched on the plush blue antique sofa, hair poufed out to here, with nails, makeup, and outfit perfectly coordinated. She looked like a lotus blossom sitting next to George, a perfect foil, but completely herself. It was the most relaxed I was ever to see her. Tammy was sweet, in the way that only Southern women can be sweet, and a bundle of nerves. I don't think she ever got over her ascendancy from the beauty parlor. At times it could seem as if she were merely a vehicle for her Voice, which had ambitions of its own, occasionally overreaching her own personal understanding of her goals. I remember driving by Tammy's house in Nashville and staring at the wrought-iron gates with FIRST LADY ACRES scrolled across the top. I would think of her—proud but not egotistical (a feat in itself), delicate and strong—and of how the world would never again be innocent enough to produce another Tammy Wynette.

In the early days of my own career I may have spent too much time around Emmylou. Her voice became a template for me, but it was one I could never hope to replicate or even approach. I did not have the high, lonesome, elegiac tone, the pierce and warble, the crystal beauty, the tears under the snow. My own instrument was darker and roomier, damp and yearning, something more untamed and imperfect. It took me a long time to let go of viewing Emmylou as a model and getting down to business with what I had. I remained fiercely critical of my own singing for many years, which wore holes in my confidence and stamina. Content mirrored context.

I went on performing in the shadow of these great role models, and more—Linda Ronstadt, Joni Mitchell, Grace Slick, Janis Joplin, Judy Collins, Laura Nyro—always questioning, always judging my own instrument, until one day in August of 1998, at a gallery opening I attended with John. I began to talk to someone in the crowd when I discovered I could not be heard because I was unable to get my voice above a rasp. As we walked out, John remarked, "Your voice has been like that for a few weeks. You should get it checked out." I said it was probably allergies and forgot about it, as I was more concerned at the time about being four months' pregnant and still suffering miserably from morning sickness. September passed, and my voice did not get better. I had a show scheduled for the following month—a big benefit for a hospital in California—and as the date approached, I grew more and more worried about my voice. I drank teas with honey, took various lozenges, sprayed it, gargled it, and doused it, but I sounded more and more like Tom Waits with a bad cold. The day of the show came and I was nearly mute. I went out onstage, praying that a miracle would happen and my voice would reappear just in time. After croaking my way through a few songs, I exasperatedly asked the crowd of hospital administrators, "Is there a doctor in the house?"

I made an appointment with Dr. Gwen Korovin, an ENT who takes care of singers. She put a camera down my throat, and when the image appeared on the screen, she stepped back as if someone had jumped in front of her. I had polyps, and they were huge, covering the entire left side of my vocal cords. Gwen stammered that she had not seen polyps this large on someone who had not been a heavy lifetime smoker, so she did not understand it. (She was certain, gratifyingly, that I did not have cancer.) While puzzled, she knew for certain that they had to be removed, and we scheduled surgery for six months after the birth of my baby, who was due in January.

As my pregnancy progressed, I grew even hoarser. Gwen checked my vocal cords shortly before I gave birth and shook her head. "The bigger you get, the bigger the polyps get," she said.

I gave birth to my and John's son, Jake, in January. I was overjoyed that at the age of forty-three I had given birth naturally to a healthy eight-pound baby boy, but I was bereft that I could not even sing him a lullaby. In March, Gwen attended a conference in Paris, where a husband-and-wife team (an obstetrician and an ENT) gave a talk on hormones and polyps. Gwen spoke to them about my case after their presentation. "Don't operate," they urged her. "The polyps will go away when her hormones return to normal, after breastfeeding." During the fourteen months I nursed him, I had my doubts that I would ever have a voice again, but they were right: Six months after that, the polyps had disappeared. But my voice was a mess. Gwen sent me to William Riley, a vocal coach and voice therapist, to rebuild it. I was terrified when I started to sing for him that he would tell me it was useless, that my voice was irreparably damaged, but at the end of an hour he said, "You're just seriously out of shape. You can get it back." We spent the next year rebuilding my voice from scratch. During those long, frightening days of near-muteness, I vowed that if my voice ever returned, I would give up the internal monologue of self-criticism about it. I promised myself that I would enjoy it, for a change. And I did. I saw my voice in a whole new way once I really did get it back. It was so much stronger than I had believed, so much more lithe and nuanced. It was like meeting an old friend who I had not appreciated in my youth but who became a close and cherished companion in my middle age.

Jakob William Leventhal was born on January 22, 1999. I thought I knew just about everything there was to know about parenting after twenty-plus years of motherhood, but what I knew about was mothering girls. I had never believed that raising boys could be that different, but I soon discovered how wrong I was. I have grown to deeply love and respect the emotional singularity of the male psyche, particularly after decades of trying to navigate the complex and exhausting tunnels and curves of the inner lives of women: my daughters' and my own. Jake keeps his own counsel. He is refreshingly transparent, but that is not to say he is one-dimensional. He has a remarkable sensitivity to music—to pitch, tempo, and song structure—which has been apparent in him since he was a toddler, when he would stand flailing at his plastic guitar in front of an armoire so he could hear the sound bounce off its surface. He is exceptionally even-tempered in a family with a lot of girls who incline toward the dramatic and convoluted in their emotional lives. He brought that with him when he was born—it was nothing I taught him. He has a dignity to his emotions that has inspired me to refine my own expression of feeling. In fact, I am certain I have become more circumspect about what I am willing to share with others because of his elegant example of judicious communication. I have to be careful not to make him a confidant or too close a friend; I remind myself that no matter how much apparent wisdom and self-regard he has in his emotional portfolio, he still needs a mother.

One day when he was four, he and I went to visit John at the recording studio on Gansevoort Street. When we left, it was bitterly cold. I couldn't find his gloves, so I took mine off and put them on his hands. He looked up at me, confused. "But what about your hands?" he asked.

"It's my job to take care of you right now," I told him cheerfully. He looked down uncomfortably. I could tell he still felt uneasy and a little worried about my cold hands.

"Someday when I'm old and you're a grown man, if I forget my gloves, you can lend me yours. Okay?" I smiled at him. He nodded, reassured, and we went on our way. My heart ached to witness his native compassion.

Although I was forty-three when I gave birth to Jake, I didn't suffer unduly while carrying him or giving birth (except for a wicked and months-long postepidural headache, which turned out to be related to a then undiagnosed brain condition). It was, in fact, the perfect emotional age to have a baby. All the anxiety about balancing work and motherhood, about my own merits as a mother, about what was right for him, or right for me, dissipated. I knew what to do, and I was thrilled to do it. In a bittersweet way, losing the baby in the first year of my marriage to John enabled me to parent Jake from a context of pure gratitude. At his tenth birthday party, as I was setting up the balloons and the Lego party favors and the cupcakes, I overheard Hannah say to Chelsea, "Can you believe Mom is *still* doing the birthday cupcakes?" They shook their heads in sympathetic fatigue. I laughed. Thirty years of the birthday cupcakes. It's a privilege.

I had begun recording a new album the summer of 1998, with John producing, and though we continued working as long as we could, we eventually shelved the project when it became clear that I could not sing at all. We picked up where we had left off after I began vocal work with Bill Riley. Although I had already written or cowritten eight out of the eleven songs I planned to record, I wanted to cast a net for some outside material, so preoccupied had I been first with trying to get pregnant and then with staying pregnant and feeling awful, and so frustrated at picking up the guitar when I couldn't sing at all. We asked Craig Northey, from the Canadian band the Odds, and Joe Henry to contribute songs for the record. Craig sent "Beautiful Pain," and Joe a song he cowrote with Jakob Dylan, "Hope Against Hope." They were both great songs and a pleasure to sing, but the most fortuitous thing to come out of that commission was that I made two good friends in Craig and Joe. Joe and I have grown very close; he is a constant source of inspiration to me.

I had composed a chorus for a song called "Rules of Travel" years earlier, and though I had tried dozens of different melodies for the verses, I could never make it work; I could never even find exactly what I wanted to convey in the verses. Hearing me struggling with the song yet again, John finally said, "This is one of the best choruses you've written. You have to finish it." We finished it together, and decided it would be the title of the album.

While driving on the Long Island Expressway a few years before, in a haze of anxiety about my dad, who was then suffering yet another health crisis, I had written the lyrics to "September When It Comes" and put them in my purse. Eventually that piece of paper found its way to the third floor of our brownstone, where John picked it up. "What is this?" he asked. "This is really good." He took the lyrics and wrote the melody, a mournful and exquisite piece of music.

I recorded "September When It Comes" when we came back to the project after the return of my voice. Listening to the completed track pensively, John observed, "You really should ask your dad to sing on this with you, as a duet." I demurred, and when he brought the idea up again a few weeks later, again I declined. Several months passed and John said, "If ever there was a song or a time to do a duet with your father, this is the song and this is the time." I suddenly knew he was right.

I called my dad and said, "Dad, I have this song, and I was wondering if you'd sing on it."

He was silent for a moment and then said, "I'll have to read the lyrics first." I laughed and told him I'd deliver them in person.

I flew to Nashville with the lyrics and the audio files, and after reading the words to the song, he nodded. "I could do this," he said quietly. He knew it was about his own mortality, about closing the door on the past, about what can never be resolved, only endured.

We went over to the cabin in the woods near his house, where he had his recording studio, accompanied by my brother, John Carter, who would record Dad's vocal. Dad clearly wasn't feeling well at all, so I gave him an out: "Dad, you don't have to do this. We can do it another time."

"No," he said firmly. "I want to try it."

As he learned the song, he got stronger with every take. I stood listening on the other side of the glass of the vocal booth, tears rolling down my face. We recorded three separate takes, and then he said, "You take that back to New York, and if John says it isn't good enough, I'll do it again."

"It's good enough, Dad," I told him, laughing. "I promise you."

When Al Gore spoke at Dad's funeral on September 15, six months after the record was released, he mentioned the song in his eulogy and its strange prescience. "It's September," he intoned, and nodded at me.

When I was a child, I remember sitting in my fourth-grade Catholic school class and figuring out how old I would be at the turn of the century. It seemed unlikely to me then that I would live to be as old as forty-five at the dawn of the new millennium, not to mention absolutely inconceivable that I had a future as a middle-aged woman. I nonetheless placed those figures in my mental files and kept them there safely for years. In about 1998 I retrieved my childhood estimates and was startled to realize that my ten-year-old self had not allowed for the fact that I wouldn't turn forty-five until May of that year, so I would actually be forty-four on January 1, 2000. I felt an unsettling ripple reach backward in time, to my fourth-grade classroom, freeing both my current and childhood selves. Having realized that I had been operating on a false premise for over thirty years, I now felt a palpable sense of relief. Maybe some of the other burdens I had carried from the past into my adult life had also been based on equally false assumptions, and maybe I could review some of them now, find a fatal flaw in my logic, revise my prospects for the future, make my way through my personal mazes, and put away some of my regrets and obsessions. It was never too late to undo who you had become.

·   ·   ·   ·   ·

My earliest memory, perhaps the earliest possible flawed template for my life, dates to when I was around two years old. We were visiting my mother's parents in San Antonio, and my grandfather, Tom, the bespectacled insurance agent, master amateur magician, renowned rose breeder, and champion gin rummy player, took me to the park to feed the pigeons. He was sitting on a green bench, tossing seeds from a bag to the birds, which were flocking around his feet. He kept saying, "Look at the birds, Rosanne!" and I thought to myself, with a sharp clarity that I now spend most of my waking hours trying to recapture, *Oh, I am supposed to pretend to be excited. I am supposed to act like a child.* And so I did. I squealed obligingly, feigned alarm at the gathering birds, and pleased my grandfather. It was a bad way to start things off, actually—a compelling need to please people can be deadly.

In 1961, when we lived in Los Angeles, my father and I both suffered from respiratory problems. Even then, the air pollution there was significant, and that was why he'd decided to move us north to Casitas Springs, where the air was crystal clear and desert clean. I don't think he even noticed how miserable the little town itself was, so pleased was he with the idea of owning his own small mountain, with absolute privacy and a desert climate. The only problem was that by the time he had the big ranch-style house built and moved us in, he was spiraling into his own extended experiment in chaos, self-destruction, and addiction, as well as constantly traveling.

Once, when I was about nine years old, my dad accidentally set fire to the mountain with a spark from the tractor he was riding. I called the fire department myself and said in the most adult and calm voice I could manage, "I just want you to know that Johnny Cash's house is on fire." The woman's voice at the other end replied, very formally, "We've received the message." For years I wondered whether she had given me the formal, scripted, official response to every report of a fire, or whether a dozen—or twenty, or fifty— people who lived down below in Casitas Springs, obviously deliri- ous with excitement from the sight of the entire mountain in flames and the prospect of a celebrity's house being consumed at any mo- ment, had already notified the fire department, and the woman, weary from the flood of calls, had formulated a rote response that was short and to the point. I remember the feel of the smoke in my lungs that lingered for days afterward: the sensation of heaviness in my chest, the trouble and pain it caused me to take a breath. From my current perspective, with Mom and Dad dead and my sisters scattered to every far corner of the country and everyone who'd ever lived in Casitas Springs in the 1960s surely dead or relocated, I think that if I had had the presence of mind as a nine-year-old, I would have told Dad to just finish the job, burn the whole moun- tain, and save us all a lot of unnecessary psychic torment on that lonely, arid, snake-infested hillside.

In 1979, I checked my guitar, a Martin D-28, at the curb at LAX on my way to Hawaii to begin my honeymoon with Rodney, which had been delayed for three weeks while I was finishing my first album for Columbia. I waited at the little outdoor baggage claim in Lihue for my guitar to come off the carousel, but it never did. Rodney became alarmed even earlier than I did, and began saying, "I don't think your guitar is going to show up." Even when it was clear that it was missing, even after we had filed the missing luggage report, I still felt fairly confident that it would appear. Thirty-six years later, I am still waiting for that guitar to turn up. It had been a gift from my dad, who had inserted a handwritten note into its sound hole saying something to the effect that it was a present from him to me, his daughter, with love, along with the date.

Somewhere, someone has my guitar and knows damn well it belongs to me. Since the advent of the Internet, I have made half-hearted attempts to find it. I have alerted my friend Matt Umanov, of the legendary eponymous guitar store in Greenwich Village, to the style, color, and year of the instrument, and he has promised to keep a lookout. I have an illogical but certain belief that my guitar will be returned to me before I die, even if I am ninety years old and have only a week to live. I just know I will see that guitar again. I am counting on it. If my dad, from his perch in the other world, wanted to do something really great for me, he might hasten its return. I'm sure he knows where it is by now.

I went to so many funerals over the course of six months in 2003 that I eventually developed a relationship with the directors of the funeral home in Hendersonville, Tennessee, where my father, my stepmother, my stepsister, and my aunt were dressed and laid out before they were buried in the cemetery right across the parking lot. I spent a lot of time in those offices, making decisions with my siblings about the color of caskets, the wording of obituaries, the size of headstones. Weight of heart. Look of future. Lack of answers.

One horrible day in a long string of horrible, macabre days that year, while I was walking down the wide hall between the individual "parlors" of the funeral home, one of the directors stopped me to inquire about my own plans for the disposition of my body after my demise, and whether they might "take care of me," since they now had such an enduring professional relationship with my entire family.

"No, thank you," I replied, shuddering. "I'm not going into the ground. I want to be cremated."

He became instantly alert and focused. "Would you like to be a diamond?"

"Excuse me?"

"There's a lot of new technology. You can have your body reduced to carbon and turned into a diamond."

I paused. "Let me ask my daughters if one of them would be interested in wearing me around her neck, and I'll let you know."


At June's funeral I wore a black Jil Sander suit with a knee-length skirt and collarless jacket, one of the most expensive items of clothing I had ever purchased. I had bought it a few months earlier under the assumption that I would be wearing it to my dad's funeral, as he was back in the hospital and we were all frantic with worry. Dad recovered, so I wore the suit, along with black satin Prada shoes and a black satin wide-brimmed hat, to bury June.

I carried one of her old handbags as I delivered her eulogy in the cavernous modern Baptist church in Hendersonville:

*Many years ago, I was sitting with June in the living room at home, and the phone rang. She picked it up and started talking to someone, and after several minutes I wandered off to another room, as it seemed she was deep in conversation. I came back ten or fifteen minutes later, and she was still completely engrossed. I was sitting in the kitchen when she finally hung up, a good twenty minutes later. She had a big smile on her face, and she said, "I just had the nicest conversation," and she started telling me about this other woman's life, her children, that she had just lost her father, where she lived, and on and on. . . . I said, "Well, June, who was it?" and she said, "Why, honey, it was a wrong number."*

*That was June. In her eyes, there were two kinds of people in the world: those she knew and loved, and those she didn't know and loved. She looked for the best in everyone; it was a way of life for her. If you pointed out that a particular person was perhaps not totally deserving of her love, and might in fact be somewhat of a lout, she would say, "Well, honey, we just have to lift him up." She was forever lifting people up. It took me a long time to understand that what she did when she lifted you up was to mirror the very best parts of you back to yourself. She was like a spiritual detective: She saw into all your dark corners and deep recesses, saw your potential and your possible future, and the gifts you didn't even know you possessed, and she "lifted them up" for you to see. She did it for all of us, daily, continuously. But her great mission and passion were lifting up my dad. If being a wife were a corporation, June would have been the CEO. It was her most treasured role. She began every day by saying, "What can I do for you, John?" Her love filled up every room he was in, lightened every path he walked, and her devotion created a sacred, exhilarating place for them to live out their married life. My daddy has lost his dearest companion, his musical counterpart, his soul mate and best friend.*

*The relationship between stepmother and children is by definition complicated, but June eliminated the confusion by banning the words "stepchild" and "stepmother" from her vocabulary, and from ours. When she married my father in 1968, she brought with her two daughters, Carlene and Rosie. My dad brought with him four daughters: Kathy, Cindy, Tara, and me. Together they had a son, John Carter. But she always said, "I have seven children." She was unequivocal about it. I know, in the real time of the heart, that that is a difficult trick to pull off, but she was unwavering. She held it as an ideal, and it was a matter of great honor to her.*

*When I was a young girl at a difficult time, confused and depressed, with no idea of how my life could unfold, she held a picture for me of my adult self: a vision of joy and power and elegance that I could grow into. She did not give birth to me, but she helped me give birth to my future. Recently, a friend was talking to her about the historical significance of the*

*Carter Family, and her remarkable place in the lexicon of American music. He asked her what she thought her legacy would be. She said softly, "Oh, I was just a mother."*

*June gave us so many gifts, some directly, some by example. She was so kind, so charming, and so funny. She made up crazy words that somehow everyone understood. She carried songs in her body the way other people carry red blood cells— she had thousands of them at her immediate disposal; she could recall to the last detail every word and note, and she shared them spontaneously. She loved a particular shade of blue so much that she named it after herself: "June-blue." She loved flowers and always had them around her. In fact, I don't ever recall seeing her in a room without flowers: not a dressing room, a hotel room, certainly not her home. It seemed as if flowers sprouted wherever she walked. John Carter suggested that the last line of her obituary read: "In lieu of donations, send flowers." We put it in. We thought she would get a kick out of that.*

*She treasured her friends and fawned over them. She made a great, silly girlfriend who would advise you about men and take you shopping and do comparison tastings of cheesecake. She made a lovely surrogate mother to all the sundry musicians who came to her with their craziness and heartaches. She called them her babies. She loved family and home fiercely. She inspired decades of unwavering loyalty in Peggy and her staff. She never sulked, was never rude, and went out of her way to make you feel at home. She had tre-*

*mendous dignity and grace. I never heard her use coarse language, or even raise her voice. She treated the cashier at the supermarket with the same friendly respect that she treated the president of the United States.*

*I have many, many cherished images of her. I can see her cooing to her beloved hummingbirds on the terrace at Cinnamon Hill in Jamaica, and those hummingbirds would come, unbelievably, and hang suspended a few inches in front of her face to listen to her sing to them. I can see her lying flat on her back on the floor and laughing as she let her little granddaughters brush her hair out all around her head. I can see her come into the room with her hands held out, a ring on every finger, and say to the girls, "Pick one!" I can see her dancing with her leg out sideways and her fist thrust forward, or cradling her autoharp, or working in her gardens.*

*But the memory I hold most dear is of her two summers ago on her birthday in Virginia. Dad had orchestrated a reunion and called it Grandchildren's Week. The whole week was in honor of June. Every day the grandchildren read tributes to her, and we played songs for her and did crazy things to amuse her. One day, she sent all of us children and grandchildren out on canoes with her Virginia relations steering us down the Holston River. It was a gorgeous, magical day. Some of the more urban members of the family had never even been in a canoe. We drifted for a couple of hours, and as we rounded the last bend in the river to the place where we would dock, there was June, standing on the shore in the little clearing between the trees. She had gone ahead in a car to surprise us and welcome us at the end of the journey. She was wearing one of her big flowered hats and a long white skirt, and she was waving her scarf and calling, "Helloooo!" I have never seen her so happy.*

*So, today, from a bereft husband, seven grieving children, sixteen grandchildren, and three great-grandchildren, we wave to her from this shore, as she drifts out of our lives. What a legacy she leaves; what a mother she was. I know she has gone ahead of us to the farside bank. I have faith that when we all round the last bend in the river, she will be standing there on the shore in her big flowered hat and long white skirt, under a June-blue sky, waving her scarf to greet us.*

For Dad's funeral I chose a black knee-length Armani skirt and a Philippe Adec jacket with sweet black-on-black appliqué flowers on one shoulder. I wore black stockings and the same Prada satin pumps, which still had bits of dried mud on them from June's funeral four months before.

I fainted at the funeral home. I came to on the floor with my aunt shaking some sense into me and my husband yelling at me to breathe. Tara waited until I was on my feet and fully conscious and then reprimanded me, and rightly so. "Get a grip. Your children are here," she said.

The eulogy I delivered at his funeral, in the same vast church, was not nearly as articulate as the one I wrote for June, since over the course of the previous four months I had lost a good deal of the natural grace and power of my vocabulary:

*I have no words that can say who he is, or what we feel.*

*But on behalf of Kathy, Cindy, Tara, John Carter, and myself, we mourn with the very essence of mourning the loss of two connected but separate Beings: Johnny Cash and Daddy. The larger-than-life qualities of this luminous soul—his poetry, his voice, his compassion and humility, his pure love and equally pure pain—if those qualities were distilled down to a series of small, private, and precious moments, that is where we found our daddy. It was not the scope of his artistry and his remarkable body of work which made him great. He was already great. The music just came out of it. He was not famous when he taught us to water-ski, or fish, or how to make ice cream out of snow. He was not a performer when he walked us down the aisle or stood by us at our weddings, or sang his special song reserved for his newborn grandbabies (which went, "Boom-ba-ba-Boom, Boom-ba-ba-Boom . . ."). He was not an icon when he told us how he loved us, how beautiful and handsome we were, how proud he was. He never criticized, he never condescended to us, never forced his will on us, never raised his voice or lectured. He offered advice only when we asked for it, and then he would measure his words with respect and kindness. He respected us as much as we respected him. He was so modest and humble, and so willing to live with the weight of his own pain without making anyone else pay for it.*

*He was a Baptist with the soul of a mystic.*

*He was a poet who worked in the dirt.*

*He was an enlightened Being who was racked with the suffering of addiction and grief.*

*He was real, whole, and more alive to the subtleties of this world and the worlds beyond than anyone I have known or even heard of.*

*He was the stuff of dreams, and the living cornerstone of our lives.*

*I can almost live with the idea of a world without Johnny Cash, because in truth there will never BE a world without him. His voice, his songs, the image of him with his guitar slung over his back, all that he said and sang and strummed changed us and moved us and is in our collective memory and is documented for future generations.*

*I cannot, however, even begin to imagine a world without Daddy.*

*The best thing I could wish for him now is that all his beliefs are coming true.*

For my stepsister Rosey's funeral, six weeks after my dad's, I wore a short, black felt wool Club Monaco skirt, my twenty-year-old Yohji Yamamoto collarless jacket, black tights, and knee-high boots. I could not face the satin Prada pumps one more time. Her widower spoke to the congregation, in the modest funeral home parlor, about the vast quantities of drugs Rosey liked to ingest, and proceeded to tell the story, infamous in our family, of the Thanksgiving dinner when Rosey was asked by her mother what she would like as a gift for Christmas that year. She replied, staring at my brother without a trace of humor, "I guess I'd like a penis, because that's the only way anybody gets any attention around here." It was at that moment in the service that I decided that an extemporaneous eulogy was in order. Leaning over to my sister and brother to tell them I was going to speak, I quickly got up out of the pew. I don't remember what I said then; I just wanted them to forget what *he* had said. I was utterly exhausted. I absolutely could not take anymore, I remember thinking, with some anger. This was not a taunt to some higher power to see how serious I was about having reached my limit, but it was perhaps taken that way, as things turned out.

In 1977, I was on a flight from Munich to Montego Bay. There were a few legs to the trip: Munich to Frankfurt, Frankfurt to New York, New York to Jamaica. My dad and June were already at Cinnamon Hill, where I planned on joining them for a few weeks of vacation. When the plane stopped in New York, an agent from the airline got on and came to my seat.

"Miss Cash? We have a message from your father in Jamaica. He says to tell you to get off the plane. There is a hurricane in the Caribbean, and he is concerned about your safety."

I got off the plane. I had only about a dollar in my purse. Fortunately, I had a single credit card, which apparently worked, and which I used to check into a hotel near JFK, where I waited a couple of days for the hurricane to pass before getting back on a plane to Jamaica.

That little incident might well stand as representative of what happened to me constantly when I was coming of age, which I recall as a series of bizarre interruptions, rapid changes of plans, stops and starts, occasional great events, and temporary but intense confusion. I was always without money, but somehow I managed to travel the world first-class; find comfortable places to live and unusual, interesting people to stay with and go out with to restaurants and music clubs; sign contracts for grand ideas; work my way into peculiar circumstances in remote locations; and generally live off the grid, and outside the normal patterns of young adult development. This template of constant change and inverse experience stayed with me through my twenties and thirties. It resonates less now, though my life is no less chaotic and full of travel, but my internal discipline and sense of structure override its influence.

In the spring of 1978, I got off a flight from Munich and was kept in customs for three hours in Los Angeles because I had failed to declare some clothing I had bought in Germany. When I finally left the airport after paying a heavy fine and having my name entered into the computer with a red flag for the next seven years, making every international trip a miserable inconvenience, I went straight to my stepsister Rosey's apartment, in a very unfashionable section of Los Angeles off La Brea Avenue. She was not at home, so I removed a window screen, forced her window open and slipped inside, took a shower, and went straight to a record release party for my stepsister Carlene at the Magic Castle in Hollywood. There I met Rodney Crowell, and that was the night that began our romance, after the unrequited love on my part, and the demos we made together that got me the Ariola contract. We remained together from that night for the next thirteen years.

· · · · ·

Then, my mother. My youngest sister and I sat with her body, alone, for an hour after she died, both of us surprised that the nursing staff let us remain. I went with my stepdad, Dick, to pick out the casket and the headstone, wrote the inscription for the headstone, and submitted it for my sisters' approval. I went to the funeral home with all of them and decided on the format of the services, I agreed to the autopsy, and I wrote another eulogy. By now both the Armani and the Jil Sander were out of the question, as none of my clothes fit properly. I was swollen with shock and fear. I wore pearls and an old black blazer and a black skirt that was coming apart at the seams, and I resurrected the damnable black satin Prada pumps. I got them out just a few days ago, and they are still encrusted with mud.

The last eulogy I wrote was for my mom, on May 24, 2005. I delivered it at Sacred Heart, her longtime parish in Ventura:

*My mother was a gardener. She loved flowers and plants and everything that bloomed, and everything that bloomed loved her back. All of nature seemed to blossom in her presence. She had no prejudice—she treated the industrial boxwood or hedges with the same care as the fragile orchid or the jasmine, or her prize roses. I always stood in awe of what my mother could do with things that grew in the earth. It seemed that just her presence had an energizing and nurturing effect. And so it was with us, her children. During our fragile moments, our struggles, and our dark nights of the soul, she treated us with the extra care she would a hothouse orchid. She was attentive, and kind, and gave just the right amount of nurturing—not too much to suffocate, or too little to starve. When we were wayward and rebellious, or ill-mannered and negligent, she was not afraid to prune us like an errant vine with the authority of her voice and command;* she *was the gardener and we would grow according to her design. The plant did not talk back to the gardener. And how grateful we are for that today, as grown women with children of our own.*

*When I woke this morning, my husband and I were talking about the difficult day ahead, and about my mother and her legacy to us. And John said, "Your mother was the definition of a life well spent. She was always engaged, in her children, her friends, her faith, and her whole community. It's inspiring. That's how we all should live."*

*It's so true. I can look at the beauty in my life, the sacred space of my home, and the faith in my heart, and witness the love, consideration, and good manners of my children, and I have to thank my mother. She taught me how to do that. She taught me how to find the beauty, how to teach the child, how to be fierce and loyal, how to love unconditionally, and how to be happy—which by itself is an extraordinary gift. There was no higher calling to her than making a home and being a wife and mother. She was as devoted and confident as a wife, first to my father for thirteen years and then to Dick for thirty-eight years, as she was as a mother. And then, as a grandmother, she was exalted. She filled in all the gaps, she ordered their universe on a foundation of love.*

*When I was a teenager, my home was always open to my friends, at any time of day or night. My mother never required advance notice or permission. She was always effusive in her welcome, interested in our lives, entertained by our teenage wackiness, and, if we went too far, as my friend Peggy and I did when we left school one day and took an impromptu trip to Mexico, she was imperial in her fury. I was grounded for months. Thank you for that, Mom.*

*My mother was the source of endless love and constant devotion, but she was also the immovable wall, the firm limit and the guiding light, until we were wise enough to provide those things for ourselves. Some of us took longer than others, even well into adulthood, but she never wavered in her example of strength and wisdom, and in her belief that we would show up clean, perfectly groomed, well mannered, and a productive and vital member of society. I will spend my life with those expectations ever in front of me, and thank God, and Mom, for that.*

*My mother died on my fiftieth birthday. The day before, I saw it coming. I could see where she was headed, and I was devastated at the symbolism, which I could not even begin to understand. I could not imagine why her soul, and her plan with God, included linking her departure from this earth with the day I was born. I felt as if I were in a dark cave, groping at the walls for direction and meaning. Over the last few days, I have begun to get a glimmer of understanding, although it may take the rest of my life to fully decode the profound message she gave me. She loved birthdays. They were extraordinarily important to her—not just the birthdays of her husband and children, but her own birthday, and that of her extended family and friends, even acquaintances. She remembered the birthdays of people who were long passed, or people she hadn't seen in years. She would remark that it was someone's birthday, and oftentimes we wouldn't even know who that person was. In fact, I know that she had birthday cards carefully signed and addressed to different people, for Dick to send out after she was admitted to the hospital. The day of a person's birth was significant to her, even if the person was only marginal in her life.*

*She died on Tuesday, May 24, almost to the hour of the moment she gave birth to me fifty years ago. She completed a magnificent circle, in perfect symmetry. She had a career as a mother of exactly fifty years, to the hour. She let us know, in no uncertain terms, that she defined herself as a mother, that it was her great passion and her proudest accomplishment, and we will never be allowed to forget that, because her passing is permanently linked to the moment she became a mother. It is written in stone now. It is written in our hearts, as well. I feel humbled by the distinction and the honor that my mother's soul was born into heaven on the day I was born into the world. And I also know she's saying, "I did my job, baby. Fifty years is long enough. Time for me to rest, now."*

*An old Eskimo poem reads:*

*Perhaps the light in the sky is not stars,*
*but rather openings in heaven*
*where the love of our lost ones pours through*
*and shines down upon us to let us know they are happy.*

*I will spend the rest of my life standing under the stars to feel her happiness, and her love. And on those nights which are dark, devoid of available light, I have only to look to the ground to see her presence, in the roses and hibiscus, the hedges and the vines, the flowering plants and everything green and blossoming that grows in the earth, that she loved and touched and made to grow, just like my sisters, just like me.*

The eulogy was too sentimental for my taste, but then, so at times was my mother.

Whenever I see a sky full of pink and gold, I always wonder how it would look at the ocean—specifically, at Indian Wells Beach in Amagansett, on Long Island. Shortly after my father died, I went there, still cracked open and hurting, with my son, Jake. It was late afternoon, with the sun very low on the horizon and the sky full of big, important-looking black clouds. The beach was empty except for a few teenagers hanging out by the lifeguard's stand, energized by the coming storm. Occasional beams of white sunlight came through the narrow alleys between the clouds and caught the tips of the waves, making them shine and the sand glow for just an instant. Ahead of me, Jake was singing to himself and skipping alongside the edge of the water, in a kind of side-to-side way, his arms out and his little gangly legs trying to keep in rhythm with the rest of his body. Heavy with sadness, I looked up to see his little body akimbo, moving like a stuttering windmill, oblivious to the impending storm, in perfect happiness. I stopped cold. *This is how my dad lives on,* I thought. Actually, I didn't even think it—I just heard the words: This is how he lives on.

I did not have many epiphanies like this after my mother died. The grief I felt for her was a blow and a grind, a dullness that fell over my waking hours and left me numb and sleepless through the night. I could not seem to shake myself into alertness from the shock of her loss. The loss of my dad, in contrast, was all sharp angles and revelatory thoughts, transformative power and energy, and gut-wrenching sorrow. I had expected his death. For almost a decade I had traveled to his hospital bed again and again, watching helplessly as he weathered catastrophic infections, terrible setbacks, and an alarming decline over the five years preceding his death. In some way this had enabled me to prepare myself. In the months after his death, I lost fifteen pounds just from moving the energy of his loss through my body. With the emotional and mental incoherence I faced after the passing of my mom twenty months later, I gained it all back.

I have taken every sorrow of my life to the ocean—the deaths of my parents, my grandparents, my aunts and uncles, friends who died untimely deaths, my stepsister Rosey and my best friend from eighth grade, the baby that never came to term, the broken relationships, divorce, the terror of the addictions of those I love— I have taken all of it to the sea. I have performed many rituals of release while immersed in salt water or walking on the shore. The ocean, for me, is what those in twelve-step programs call a Higher Power.

Looking back, I see that what I regarded as templates were merely incidents in a long life, and the only crippling potential they possessed was that which I gave them. There is not meaning in everything, but one can ascribe meaning to anything. Therein is the beauty. I gave an old man the pleasure of thinking he had introduced me to birds, by being deceptively innocent, by acting a part, but I was wrong in thinking I had to live the rest of my life that way. I watched the mountain around my childhood home burn to cinders, not realizing I was taking particular and meticulous note of exactly what I did not want for my future, in geography, climate, and community, and so, eventually, I moved to New York City, my true home. The guitar was taken, but the stolen jewelry was returned by a more loving source. I was flagged in the customs watch list, but from then on I declared everything, and not just the clothing I purchased. "I declare": a great Southernism, and a poetic way to live. I never went into a house through a window again, and afterward so many doors were opened to me. Thirteen years after the Magic Castle, I got a divorce, but I got four daughters, and I learned how to be a mother to daughters; then I remarried and learned how to be a mother to a son. I got off the plane, and avoided the hurricane.

I had lost my parents. There was no ultimately fortunate conundrum there, or if there was, I hadn't yet come to perceive it. But the footsteps of a little dancing boy cast long shadows, and pointed to new futures, where there are no templates, and dissembling and deception are not required.

n the last year of my dad's life, all his organ systems started failing. He was ravaged by diabetes and neuropathy, which was complicated by various other ailments that arose from a lifetime of hard living. He had very little healthy lung tissue left because of dozens of bouts of pneumonia and bronchitis during the previous decade. Several months before he died, he had a bad time with his feet, due to complications of the diabetes, and for a time it looked as if a toe might have to be amputated. I was aghast, and concerned that this would plunge him into a depression. I carefully asked him how he felt about it and if he was anxious about the possibility of losing a toe. He scoffed, "Nah, the one they want to take off is my least favorite toe."

It was in early 2003 that I began to lose a lot of people close to me in a very short time, starting with my aunt Louise, my father's elder sister and the matriarch of the Cash family since the death of my grandmother. Around the time of her passing, I wrote the song "Black Cadillac." The words and music both came quickly, and when I finished it, a chill came over me when I realized that it wasn't actually about Aunt Louise, but about my father. I had had the experience earlier of writing myself postcards from the future. Creative work sometimes fosters a prescience—not a psychic premonition, but rather a release from linear time, a fluidity of movement on the continuum. I knew that "Black Cadillac" had been inspired from somewhere other than the present, and that realization paralyzed me with fear.

The following month, on May 15, June died, quite unexpectedly. We children held our breath throughout that spring and summer. We did not expect my father to survive that loss, as his health had already become so compromised. In August, I went to Cambridge, England, to play at the folk festival there. On a day off I climbed to the top of a church tower with Chelsea, who had accompanied me, John, and Jake to England. We looked out over the River Cam, and I had an uncanny vision: I saw the water rise up to the top of the church tower and myself and Chelsea sailing off the tower, as if we had wings. I started writing "Dreams Are Not My Home" that day with a sick foreboding.

> *The waves are breaking on the wall*
> *The queen of roses spreads her arms to fly, she falls.*
> *If I had wings I'd cut them down*
> *And live without these dreams so I could learn to love*
>     *the ground.*
> *I want to live inside the world*
> *I want to act like a real girl*
> *I want to know I'm not alone*
> *And that dreams are not my home.*

When I got back to the States in mid-August, Jake and I went to see my dad. My sister Cindy had spent a few weeks with him that summer and had just left. I knew Dad wanted company, and I was anxious to check on him. By now he was in a wheelchair, consumed with grief and physical pain. For most of the day I would sit in his little office off the bedroom and watch the news with him—I offered to buy him a new television, a flat-screen, and he agreed that it was time to trade the old one in—or read to him. I read the Book of Job, and the Psalms, and the poetry of Will Carleton, one of his favorites. I made myself get up at three thirty in the morning, when I knew he would wake, and make coffee for him, black, with artificial sweetener. (He had finally accepted the fact that he was diabetic and gave up sugar.) During these few precious hours alone in the mornings, the house was quiet and we could really talk. We would turn on CNN and discuss that day's world events, and then he went back to sleep for an hour or so until six, when the staff arrived. In the afternoons, Jake would sit at Dad's desk and draw pictures of Power Rangers for his grandpa. Dad would hold the drawings up to look at them and exclaim, "*Power* Rangers!" delightedly.

Late in the afternoon of the day before I left to go back to New York, Dad stared out the window at the lake and said sadly, "The gloaming of the day is the hardest part." I said I knew that it was. His head tilted down to his chest. "I feel so bad," he said, and that was one of the only times in my life—maybe the only time—that I ever heard him complain about his ailments. It was extraordinary, and shocking, to see his stoic resolve crumble before my eyes. "I know, Dad," I said. "I'm so sorry."

The next afternoon I went to hug him and tell him good-bye. Dad looked at me, surprised. "I didn't know you were leaving today," he said. I reminded him that I had told him I had an early evening flight to New York. "But I thought you were going to have coffee with me tomorrow morning," he said, his confusion evident in his face. My heart ached, but I pushed the feeling aside. "No, Dad, I have to go," I said. "But, remember, you're coming to New York for the MTV awards in a couple weeks, right?" "Oh, yeah," he said, and nodded. He had said that he was determined to attend the awards, as he had a few nominations, and he was going to work with a physical therapist that his producer, Rick Rubin, had recommended to help him regain his strength and get back on his feet. I could see now that he didn't actually believe he would be able to make it. His surrender alarmed me, but I pushed that feeling aside as well. I got to the airport and discovered that the blackout of 2003 had stricken New York City and much of the Northeast, and my flight was delayed indefinitely. I called Dad to ask him what CNN was saying about the blackout, and after we considered my options, I decided to wait at the airport. My flight was ultimately canceled, and I was rescheduled for one early the next morning. I debated whether to drive the forty miles back out to Dad's and spend the night, which would have meant leaving there the next morning at five a.m. I decided instead to check into an airport hotel, but I didn't tell Dad, knowing how disappointed he would be if I didn't come back to the house. It turned out that I waited at the airport most of the following day and didn't get on a flight until late that afternoon.

On September 11, I got a call from Phil Maffetone, Dad's physical therapist, to discuss his treatment and how he could build strength. At the time Phil was in the bedroom with Dad, and he suddenly stopped in the middle of our conversation to say that something was happening with Dad. Phil became alarmed and promised to call me back. An ambulance came. John Carter and his wife, Laura, phoned me from the hospital. "You'd better come," Laura said quietly. I booked the next flight, which left me only an hour to reach Newark Airport. I was beside myself with anxiety, as it was still rush hour and I knew the Holland Tunnel would surely be packed with commuters. I got a taxi, and when we reached the tunnel we discovered that it was completely empty. The driver turned fully around in his seat and stared at me in shock, as if I had something to do with it. "I've never seen it like this," he said. "Maybe because it's the anniversary of 9/11," I offered.

When I arrived at the hospital at around ten p.m., Dad was still conscious. He squeezed my hand and lifted his eyebrows to let me know that he could hear me when I spoke to him. After a few hours, everyone left except for my sister Kathy, John Carter, and me. John Carter went to lie down somewhere, and Kathy and I went across the hall to an empty ICU room. I fell asleep in a chair and awoke to the sound of Kathy crying and a nurse gently tapping my arm. We went across the hall to Dad. I sang "The Winding Stream" into his ear, and he struggled for a half hour more. He died at 1:20 a.m., September 12. I held his hand for a long time after, and the nurse cut a lock of his hair for each of us children.

We had to wait a few hours for officials to come and sign some papers, because of a rule about the verification of the cause of death of someone who has been in the hospital for less than twenty-four hours. Kathy finally went home, and in the early morning hours John Carter and I followed our father's body as it was wheeled through the labyrinthine basement recesses of the hospital. "It's like we're going to the stage," John Carter said suddenly, and the connection struck me as eerily similar and exquisitely, painfully beautiful: All of us children had followed Dad so many times through the backstage halls and mazes and basements of arenas as he made his way to the stage. He would have loved the metaphor.

I got about three hours of sleep, between three and six a.m., and then I started watching the clock. I was at peace with the fact of that day, a day on which he was still alive, albeit briefly, and I was dreading midnight, when it would become September 13, the first day on which he would be dead forever. On Friday, September 12, air had still gone in and out of his lungs; he had moved his limbs and made sounds. He had actually squeezed my hand and lifted his eyebrows. It was a difficult day, the last day of my dad's life, but not unbearable to me. The next day, the beginning of my dad in the past tense, was unbearable.

Six weeks later, when my stepsister Rosey died of carbon monoxide poisoning, I started writing the rest of the songs that would become *Black Cadillac*, out of a near-desperate need to control something in my universe amid the tidal wave of loss that seemed to keep rolling over my family. The first song I wrote after my dad's death was "God Is in the Roses," followed shortly by "The World Unseen," the opening line of which was a reference to Psalm 102, which Dad so loved and which I'd read to him several times in the last few months of his life: "I watch, and am as a sparrow alone upon the housetop."

In my song, the image became, "I'm the sparrow on the roof / I'm the list of everyone I have to lose."

It was after composing "The World Unseen" that I realized I was writing a concept record. John encouraged me to keep the lyrics grounded and somewhat literal, to focus on the houses and the birds and the waves and bells and roses, to describe the artifacts of grief rather than the specific feelings. In the midst of mourning, I had to be reminded to stay away from what I had always considered anathema to great songwriting: big themes. John wrote the music for four of the songs.

I wanted to start recording, with John as producer again, but he was in the midst of another project and it was taking months longer than we had anticipated. Julian Raymond, my A&R person, called with an idea: Would I be willing to work with Bill Bottrell, a record producer and guitarist who had a deep affinity for roots music, and let him produce a few songs? If it didn't work, I could back up and wait for John, but if it did, we could record five songs and get a head start on the project. I agreed and sent Bill a few of the songs. We did some basic preproduction, but the arrangements were still pretty much up in the air when I went to Los Angeles to work with him and the band he had put together: Dan Schwartz on bass, Brian MacLeod on drums, my old friend Benmont Tench on keyboards, and Bill himself on guitars. From the first day, it all just worked. Bill was a bit dark, a bit laconic, and I respected him and felt I understood him—and he certainly understood me, and these songs. There were moments I felt awkward to have the guys hear the rawness of the lyrics, but the feeling passed, and they took the music and the process very seriously. I went back and forth to Los Angeles three or four times to do the basic tracks and start the mixes with Bill, and the record came together very quickly. When we were about to mix the song "Black Cadillac," Julian came into the studio looking very uncomfortable. He had an idea, he explained, but before he would tell us what it was, he insisted that I could stop him and tell him to fuck off at any time. He was stumbling all over himself to get it out, but finally explained that he wanted to try to put some warped mariachi-type horns on the end of the song to echo the horns on my dad's "Ring of Fire," as a kind of homage to the content of the lyrics. I surprised myself by agreeing immediately. It turned out to be an eerie moment and a subtle reference that not everyone got, but those who did found it hauntingly effective.

Almost as soon as I was finished with Bill, John was available to start working with me, and we did the second half of the record in New York. We brought my old friend Michael Rhodes up from Nashville to play bass, and there was a sweet feeling of continuity and connection with the past through him, as he'd first played with me on *King's Record Shop* in the late eighties, and we had been very close. These sessions also went seamlessly, and I think John felt a bit like a gauntlet had been thrown with the quality of Bill's work. He rose to the occasion musically, doing his best work.

One song that John and I wrote, "House on the Lake," was full of documentary detail about my dad and June's house in Tennessee— the rose garden, the blue bedroom, the lake itself—and I became concerned that it might be too literal, as I do like poetic license and ambiguity of time and place in songwriting. I was liberated from those concerns after one of the very first times I performed the song in concert, when an acquaintance came up after the show and sighed. *"Everyone's* got his own house on the lake . . ."

After I finished the record, I came upon some old reel-to-reel tapes of my mom and dad talking to me when I was a toddler. I took the recordings to the mastering lab, where they found the necessary equipment to play the obsolete format. I began to search for a particular moment in the tapes, and found it, which allowed me to open the record with a snippet of my dad saying, "Rosanne! Say, 'Come on.'"

With time the unbearable becomes shocking, becomes sad, and finally becomes poignant. Or maybe poignancy isn't the conclusion to grief. Maybe there is something beyond poignant that I haven't experienced yet. I was able to renegotiate my inner relationship with my dad through the first few years of his absence, and much has been resolved. I hear him come on the radio in a taxi or a store, and my heart aches and is soothed at the same time. Both people I know and total strangers talk to me almost daily about their love and admiration for him. I don't resent it, even if privately I am missing him terribly, and wish I weren't constantly reminded of his absence. To let it roll over me without rancor is the best I can hope for, I think. My mother's passing, while not as public, was even more dramatic in terms of family dynamics, preemption, and mysterious numbers. She was diagnosed with lung cancer on April 22, 2005, the day before her seventy-first birthday, and she died on May 24, 2005, my fiftieth birthday. She always wanted everything to be clean, well ordered, symmetrical, and resolute. It was perfect for her. Constitutionally, she would have been destroyed by a lengthy illness and all the anxiety it entailed. She was diagnosed and gone almost in the same breath. I was her oldest child, and she connected herself to me in a mystical way, by linking her departure to my arrival.

In June the record was finished. Julian called, and it was clear that he was again trying to tell me something that was difficult for him to get out. He finally said, "If there's anything else you have to say on this record, you have six weeks."

"What do you mean?" I asked, mystified. "We've already mixed it. Hell, we've already *mastered* it, Julian."

"I'll pay to remaster it," he insisted. "If there's anything else you have to say. You have six weeks."

I hung up and within the week wrote "Like Fugitives"—about my mother's death; about the public insanity surrounding my father's death; about the forthcoming film *Walk the Line*, which had recently been previewed for me, and which I found to be an egregious oversimplification of our family's private pain, writ large and Hollywood-style; and about the torment my sisters and I were suffering from losing so many people in two years. I ended the album with a track that was seventy-one seconds of silence. To me, it was the only direct tribute track to my mother and my father, both of whom had died at the age of seventy-one.

My mother had made her exit six months before the release of the movie about our family, the idea and anticipation of which she found to be emotionally untenable. When the film was released in

America, I went to Paris to avoid the hoopla. I wandered the flea markets and the churches, went to the opera and the Grand Palais, the bistros and the shops, ate well, bought antique fabrics and topiaries, and put it completely out of my mind that there was a new version of my father's drug addiction and the collapse of my nuclear family, the two central catastrophic events of my childhood, which have cast their long shadows over my life since.

On my return to New York I steeled myself for the press I knew I would have to do to promote the record, and the inevitable and relentless obsession with the backstory. I refused to allow myself to become a poster girl for grief. I refused to let any journalist goad me into crying, which some of them certainly tried to do. I refused to discuss my last private moments with my parents, or my "feelings" about their loss. I had to develop a bit of armor to protect myself against the dozens and dozens of people who wanted me to help them process their own grief over losing my dad, some of which was genuine and some of it expressed in so many commercial ventures, whether plays, songs, books, screenplays, or concerts. I resisted, sometimes vehemently, being drawn into the experience of those who came to my concerts as if they were attending a memorial service, wearing Johnny Cash T-shirts and clutching tissues. I refused to participate in any of it, except for a single tribute concert on Country Music Television, filmed at the old Ryman Auditorium in Nashville the November after my father's death. I sang "I Still Miss Someone," with John playing guitar, and "Tennessee Flat-Top Box," with John and Randy Scruggs, reprising his original part, both of them standing next to me like sentinels of protection. The powerful aura of love and community made that night an unforgettably beautiful experience.

By the end of that oppressive six-year period, from May 2003 to June 2009, I wanted out, I wanted change, I wanted to make a record of covers that had no prescient qualities at all. *Black Cadillac* had been released in January 2006, and in the eighteen months following the release of the record, I played twenty-five concerts of a show with three narratives I had written—"Mariners and Musicians," "The Unbearable Blue," and "What Did You Dream This Time?"—and films that went with the narratives. The show was set up like a theater piece, highly structured. Danny, my manager, had a great vision for that show. It was elegiac and somewhat dark, but beautiful. Then a moody documentary film was made about me by Steven Lippman called *Mariners and Musicians* using the songs from *Black Cadillac*. It premiered at the Tribeca Film Festival. As well as the theatrical *"Black Cadillac* in Concert," I played probably fifty more shows with just John. Then I was done with it.

The tour was exhausting, and I couldn't bear to hear one more story of loss from a fan or friend, but even then, the deaths weren't over. In the three years following my mother's passing, we lost several more aunts and uncles; my sister Cindy's husband, Eddie, died in a tragic accident; and I lost two dear friends, Eric Wishnie and my songwriting mentor, John Stewart.

Three years and a couple of months after my dad died, I dreamed I was visiting one of the world's great museums, set in a lush forest at the edge of a pristine lake. Outside the museum, in a little cottage filled with light pouring through big windows, with a view of the trees and water, was a hospital bed, where my dad lay. A kind, gentle, sandy-haired doctor with spectacles was attending him. I walked in and went around the curtain shielding his bed. My dad and I acknowledged each other, and I saw that the doctor was busy with him, so I left. Dad looked ill, but still much healthier than he had been in life. When I woke up I felt relief: It was no longer my job to take care of him, as he was being taken care of, wherever he was. The legacy of his work was intact, in my dream preserved as carefully and conscientiously as if it had been in a museum. Something settled in my gut. I could let him move on now.

When I was eleven years old, we were at a lake in the mountains of Southern California—my mom, dad, sisters, my dad's sister, Aunt Reba, and her family, and a friend of my dad's, a slow-moving, laconic, tall, skinny fellow with a drawl. My mother and aunt went off on some mission, and we kids were left with the men to fish. I was walking barefoot by the picnic table when I stepped on something sharp. I didn't feel any pain, just a sudden wetness. I looked down and saw that blood was gushing from my foot into the dirt, creating a circle of dark mud around my toes. I called to my dad, who came over and bent down to look at my foot. I watched as his face went white. He quickly took off his shirt, wrapped it around my foot, and put me in the truck. My uncle stayed with the rest of the kids, and my dad's tall, skinny friend drove. As Dad explained that he was taking me to the hospital, I kept pleading, "Promise me they won't use scissors. Promise me, Daddy!" I said it over and over, and he promised each time that no scissors would be involved. Dad and I were in the ER with a doctor examining my foot when my mother walked in crying. I was still almost inconsolable before she arrived, but when I saw her tears, I understood that both of us could not be upset at the same time—it would unbalance the entire universe, with black holes materializing in hospital hallways and vortices of doom appearing at bedsides everywhere. I stopped crying.

Apparently, I had stepped on the sharp edge of an open sardine can and sliced off the end of the second toe on my right foot. The doctor was talking to my parents about skin grafts, perhaps from my thigh, when my dad's lanky friend drawled, "Well, you know, I set that sardine can up on the picnic table after I saw she stepped on it. I think that toe is still in there." Everyone stared at him, awe-struck. The doctor roused himself. "Go get it, man!"

When my mother told the story in later years, she always fin-ished by saying, her eyes glistening, "And the toe *lived!*" It was a miracle. My toe was cleaned up of sardine oil and sewn back on (scissors were involved; I was furious at my dad), and it did, indeed, live. But, sadly, it has become my least favorite toe.

In Philip Larkin's poem "An Arundel Tomb" is a line that haunts me, that hums in the background of my thoughts about my parents as they are now, in whatever place they reside: "Time has transfig-ured them into untruth."

It's not necessarily a bad thing, the untruth. Perhaps we don't get the whole truth until we can stand it, and perhaps no one can ever really stand it in the density of this physical existence. I have settled quietly on the untruth, and even found its equanimity in my daily life. In the untruth of my parents, there is still so much for me, so many acts of service, so much real impulse for goodness, no matter how thwarted or strained. I see them clearly now, flawed as they are, self-centered and driven, with incomprehensible missions and agendas, diving headlong into parenthood when they were barely out of adolescence, unsuited to the task but devoted and hopeful, and, ultimately, not even on this earth for me as much as for themselves, which is the hardest thing for a child to accept. But *how* we remember is as important as *what* we remember.

> *Time has transfigured them into*
> *Untruth. The stone fidelity*
> *They hardly meant has come to be*
> *Their final blazon, and to prove*
> *Our almost-instinct almost true:*
> *What will survive of us is love.*

September 11, 2001, was the second day of seventh grade for my youngest daughter. That day I took her to school—St. Luke's in Greenwich Village—in a taxi, as I had to attend a parents meeting in the cafeteria, which was scheduled to begin at eight thirty. As we traveled south down Seventh Avenue, I looked up and remarked to myself that I should remember a blue as fierce and dedicated as the sky was that morning, on a day that combined the best of summer and fall. It was peculiar how intense the color was above our heads, and how much I wanted to hold on to it.

Carrie went into school, and I made my way to the parents meeting, which started promptly at eight thirty. By eight forty-five I was growing a little bored and was staring dreamily at the big school clock at the front of the room when the sound of a plane suddenly filled the cafeteria, heading south, very low and very loud. Whoever was speaking at the time kept talking as the building rumbled, and I exchanged glances with some of the other mothers in the room. One woman near me said quietly, to no one in particular, "That plane is going to crash." Seconds later I heard a faint boom, like a distant construction blast. I didn't connect the two; it just seemed too far-fetched. The meeting went on, and after a few minutes passed someone came into the room and whispered to Ann Mellow, the head of the school, who was then addressing us. She listened gravely and then announced to the ten or twelve mothers and handful of teachers scattered around the tables, "A plane has crashed into the World Trade Center." I remarked to Clint, the development director, who was sitting at my table, "I bet it was that plane that went over a few minutes ago." He replied that he hadn't noticed. No one was very alarmed, as we all assumed it was a small commuter plane that had lost its way.

The meeting continued until a few moments later, when someone appeared at the door, crying, "It was a passenger jet!" We all got up and rushed out to try to find out what was happening. At the front entrance of the school I met another mother I knew, Michelle, whose husband, John Dolan, had taken the photographs of my wedding. "I just saw a second plane hit the other tower," she told me, her face alarmingly pale. I was confused. *A second plane?* I walked around the corner to the intersection of Greenwich and Christopher streets, just at the back of St. Luke's, where I had a clear view all the way downtown to the towers. I caught my breath; both were on fire. Huge, gaping black holes had been torn down the sides of both buildings. It was unnaturally quiet in the street as a small group of us stood and looked at the smoke silently billowing from the towers, almost elegant in their ruin, as if they had resigned themselves to their fate with grace. I thought to myself that without the filter, and distancing effect, of the histrionic ruminations of a newscaster, this was just too much to take in. Today, when I think about that moment and the scene I witnessed, the most unsettling part of all was the depth of the injured silence. I started crying. Robin Rue, a literary agent friend and mother of one of Carrie's classmates, came and stood next to me, and we put our arms around each other. "All this in the name of God," she said somberly. I was startled and looked at her through my tears. *Of course*, I thought. *She's absolutely right. Religion. For what other reason do people ever act with such absolute inhumanity?*

My cell phone rang, for the last time over the next three days. When I heard my mother's voice, I became a little unglued, shouting to her, "It's a terrorist attack!" I went back into the school and waited for Carrie, who was being herded with her class into the cafeteria. I took her by the arm and led her around the corner to look at the towers, and then we began walking toward our home, fifteen blocks north. I wonder now why I wanted her to see them. It felt so important to me in that moment; I was uneasy that her imagination might torture her if she didn't have the stark reality to reference. Now I'm not so sure I did the right thing. The pictures of her imagination might have been easier for her to assimilate.

The first tower fell while we were en route, and though I saw people standing on corners, staring and becoming increasingly agitated, I would not let Carrie turn around to see that, and I would not turn around to look myself. There were no available taxis. I kept trying my cell phone, with no luck, and by now the lines at pay phones were half a block long. I started to pull Carrie to hurry her along while I kept determinedly punching my home phone number into my cell phone, desperately trying to reach John, in case he had not heard the news. I wanted to warn him not to leave the house, and ask him to wait with Jake for Carrie and me to get home. A man walked by us heading south, holding a radio up on his shoulder playing very loud. "What's happening?" I asked him. "A plane hit the White House," he said, and kept walking. Though nearly paralyzed with panic, I kept dragging Carrie, and we finally got on a bus at Sixteenth Street. The other passengers were nervous, talkative, and trying their cell phones. Nothing made sense, nothing worked.

We left the bus and hurried up our block, and when I finally pulled Carrie up the stoop of our brownstone, I saw John opening the door, beside himself with worry.

"Where have you been?" he asked anxiously, pulling us into the house.

The smell of burnt plastic and toxic ash drifted up from the site and lasted well into December. Over the next several weeks the police precinct house on West Tenth Street, which was near the school, housed many extra police officers from around the country who had come and volunteered their services, and I joined a group of mothers from St. Luke's who donated food and shaving cream, shampoo, razors, and soap to them. The school received teddy bears from children all over the country who wanted to show their sympathy to the children who had witnessed such horror. The children became used to that horrible, pungent smell that hung over downtown. One day I picked Carrie up at school, and a little girl walking out next to her lifted her face to the air and exclaimed, exasperated, "It smells like the World Trade Center!" I was shocked—and comforted—by how quickly children adapt. But day after day, it continued to feel like a dream, a new life, torn from a page of the old life, with scrambled sounds and smells.

My son's first day of preschool was delayed. When Jake finally did start class, he began building towers with the blocks in his classroom and crashing a toy airplane into them to knock them down. He did this several days in a row before his teacher told me about it. I was stunned, as we had been diligent about keeping the television turned off and our emotions about it kept in check around him. Every day when I picked him up, I whispered to the teacher, "Did he do it again today?" Every day she would nod and point to the wreckage of some Legos and wooden blocks. A couple weeks went by and I finally went to the head of the school and told her that I was concerned about his behavior.

"Is he eating and sleeping all right?" she asked.

"Yes," I replied.

"Then don't worry about it," she said consolingly. "He's working it out."

After a few weeks, Jake stopped building and destroying the Lego twin towers. A few months later, early in 2002, we were heading across West Twenty-third Street in a taxi when Jake, who had been quietly looking out the window, suddenly said to me as he pointed at the view down Fifth Avenue, "Someday, all these buildings will fall down."

I resisted the impulse to believe him.

"No, honey," I assured him. "Just the two. Just the two that already fell. No more."

It took me another year before I stopped waking in the night to the sound of a jet airplane reverberating in my ears, and to the sound of my own pounding heart.

Now we New Yorkers don't talk about it. Newcomers here say they are surprised that we don't all spill our September 11 stories at the first available opportunity, but we don't. There seems to be an unacknowledged code of silence about what we each experienced that day and in the weeks that followed. We barely talk about it among ourselves. Robin Rue and I, who stood next to each other in the street and together watched the towers burn, have never discussed it since. My daughter will not allow anyone to bring up the subject. My husband and I don't speak of it. My son, now in middle school, asked about it not long ago, as if it were a made-up story he may have once heard and now wished to verify as the truth. He wanted to know why it had happened. He has no recollection of his block towers and toy airplane.

In 2007, three and a half years after my dad's death, his house burned to the ground. We had sold it to Barry Gibb and his wife, Linda, and they were in the process of an extensive renovation. A sealant being used on the wood was accidentally ignited, and the old timbers went up like newspaper. My sister-in-law Laura called me while it was happening, and I screamed as if someone had just dropped dead. My sister Kathy called me as I was talking to Laura, and gave me the cell phone number of the fire chief. (Kathy has an uncanny ability to come up with the phone number of anyone on the planet.) I called him while the house was still burning, and he was still on the site.

"This is a total loss, ma'am," he said solemnly. "I'm sorry. There will be a complete investigation, however."

The following week I went down to Nashville to present an award on television to Kris Kristofferson, my dear friend and the closest link I have to my dad now, in many ways. Country Music Television was giving him something called the Johnny Cash Visionary Award. Kris and his wife, Lisa, who were perhaps closer to Dad and June than anyone else outside the family, hired a car and driver to take me and Chelsea out to look at the damage. Each of us had our own memories of the house, and our own particular sadness about its loss. As we walked around the ruins and blackened wood, I mapped out in my head each room, each fireplace, each staircase, each light fixture, window, and door. None of what I was seeing made sense; I might have been looking at a hologram or a film set. The damage was staggering, but there was no silent rebuke in the ash and charred ruins. What I experienced was, in fact, the opposite of a rebuke— what I felt was, I realized, a benediction. I became oddly liberated, as though something difficult was finally at an end. All those fires of my youth, the mountainside my dad had set on fire with a spark from his tractor, the forest fire he had accidentally set while camping in the wilderness in California (through which he became the first individual ever sued by the state of California), the periodic wildfires that scorched the hills of Ventura and those of Malibu Canyon while I was growing up and then as a young wife and mother—all of them coalesced in this singular ruined house. I walked around the debris and fallen timbers—the single frame of a window still standing, the new view of the lake where before had been a wall—and my tears stopped. I looked at the result of this fire, and suddenly I was looking at the end of all fires. There was no re-proach, no portent of further disasters, only the conclusion of some-thing long and sad, and whatever that something was would reveal itself to me on its own, without my having to search or to struggle to understand.

In December of 2003 I traveled to Oslo for the first time since an odd little gig I had done there in 1997 in a small club for practically no money. At that time it hardly seemed a wise business decision, as I hadn't sold more than a hundred records in Oslo, and the promoter was, at best, halfhearted in his offer. But I liked the idea of Norway and its cold weather, and going only with John to play for fifty or so people with just our two guitars. As it turned out, I overestimated the size of the audience by five hundred percent. When we arrived at the club, we found a handful of Norwegian cowboys wearing tight jeans with big belt buckles and Stetson hats milling about. They clapped politely during my set and restrained themselves admirably, shouting out requests for "Ring of Fire" only a couple of times. Despite the meager attendance, John and I enjoyed ourselves, and after the show I went to the bar, where a lanky, ruddy-faced man in a black cowboy hat ambled—if Scandinavians can be said to amble—up to me.

He stared at me, unsmiling and silent. I extended my hand, a little nervously. He shook it, then said sternly, "Do you *luff* your *fater*?"

I was taken aback. "Yes," I said uncertainly.

"No!" he bellowed in response. "*I* luff your fater!" He stabbed his forefinger into his chest to accentuate his point.

On this trip I would be performing at the Nobel Peace Prize concert, as a guest of the Chieftains. A month or so before I was scheduled to leave, however, I had received an e-mail inviting me to come to Oslo a day early, to attend a concert in honor of my father by Norwegian artists, who would be performing his songs at Oslo prison. I was intrigued, to say the least. I arrived in Oslo on the morning of December 9 and that night was picked up at my hotel and taken to the prison. It was foggy and mercilessly cold as we walked through the gates and down a cobblestone path, past milky yellow lamps that diffused only slightly in the heavy fog, and then inside the thick stone walls and into the maze of the official rooms of the prison. We finally arrived at a large room where all the Norwegian artists who were to perform were waiting, some dressed in cowboy shirts and hats (articles my dad seldom wore, but people do insist on their own version of authenticity), and most wearing black.

Seated in the audience with the prisoners, I found myself crying my way through the entire concert. It was ineffably poignant to hear Dad's songs sung with such serious conviction (sometimes with slight Norwegian inflection) by musicians who were unexpectedly skilled and deeply versed in every nuance of the lexicon of Johnny Cash. At the end I was asked to say something to the audience and the performers, and I began by apologizing that I could not speak to them in their own language. A big, rough voice from the back yelled out, "It's all right!" and everyone laughed. When I returned to my hotel very late that night, I called Rick Rubin, Dad's dear friend and the producer of his "American" recordings, in Los Angeles. I told him about the concert and tried to convey how moved I was, how special it was.

"Did they record it?" he asked.

They did record the show, but I have never heard the tapes.

The Nobel Peace Prize concert, held a few days later with the Norwegian royal family and Shirin Ebadi, the peace prize recipient, in attendance, could only be described as surreal in comparison to the prison concert.

My performance with the Chieftains went well and was exciting for me, but the big finale of the show, with all the musical guests taking part, was John Lennon's "Imagine." During rehearsal Robert Plant asked me to change a line of the song—"Imagine no religion"— to avoid offending certain religious groups with whom he felt an affinity.

"But—" I said, shocked. "It's 'Imagine.' I can't change John Lennon's line!"

We argued about it very politely and decided that since I could not, on principle, change any line John Lennon had written, Robert and I would switch verses so he could have that line and could sing it as he wished while I would pretend not to notice. I don't actually remember how his version went, as I was, on the whole, out of my element. I found myself raising my arm in some melodramatic performance gesture. I was wearing a skirt and blouse— a perfectly stylish one—but not an evening gown, as the other women on the program were wearing. Throughout the night I kept thinking about the prisoners, and the Norwegian musicians, and about how in the European reversal of dates the concert in the prison happened on 9/12—December 9—which read to me as September 12, the day my dad died.

In the months since my father's passing I had come to understand that the loss of a parent expands you—or shrinks you, as the case may be—according to your own nature. If too much business is left unfinished, and guilt and regret take hold deep in the soul, mourning begins to diminish you, to constrict the heart, to truncate the vision of your own future, and to narrow the creative potential of the mind and spirit. If enough has been resolved—not everything, for everything will never be done, but just enough—then deep grief begins to transform the inner landscape, and space opens inside. You begin to realize that everyone has a tragedy, and that if he doesn't, he will. You recognize how much is hidden behind the small courtesies and civilities of everyday existence. Deep sorrow and traces of great loss run through everyone's lives, and yet they let others step into the elevator first, wave them ahead in a line of traffic, smile and greet their children and inquire about their lives, and never let on for a second that they, too, have lain awake at night in longing and regret, that they, too, have cried until it seemed impossible that one person could hold so many tears, that they, too, keep a picture of someone locked in their heart and bring it out in quiet, solitary moments to caress and remember.

Loss is the great unifier, the terrible club to which we all eventually belong.

. . . . .

A few years before he died my dad and I were in a Lowe's, a big hardware store, in Hendersonville, where he lived on the lake. I can't
remember what he needed, whether it was a tool or a filter or pool
cleaner, or maybe he didn't need anything at all. In his later years he
loved to wander the aisles of the megastores and throw things in his
cart that he would never look at again once he got home with them.
By this point he wasn't driving and he got around slowly. I had
driven him to the store, and I was following him around the aisles,
helping him carry things, and suddenly I felt the tears welling. I
don't remember what had happened, what had come up in conversation, but I stood in the aisle looking at my dad, who was staring at
me. Perhaps I just needed to know that I could let my guard down in
front of him and he wouldn't run away. Whatever he said in that
moment, it was good, it helped, it was sufficient. He reassured me,
and he tried to get me to feel better. Like most men of his generation, he was uncomfortable when women became emotional, and
he wanted to get the situation stabilized and over with as soon as
possible. I let him off the hook and gave it up pretty quickly.

We drove around for a while after leaving the hardware store,
and I listened to him talk about the beginning of his relationship
with June, how he had wrecked her Cadillac, how she had never
berated him for it, but how there were other things that still gnawed
at his heart that he had not forgotten. I barely remember what he
said then, but the opening I had given him with my tears seemed to
grant him license to express, in the most rambling way, his secret
disappointments. Even though he was only in his late sixties at the

time, he was unmistakably an old man. He had lived a long time, and he had lived a lot. He was looking back on more than most people could even imagine—four or five lives packed into one—and it had begun to exhaust him. He was fading; it was clear in the tone of his recollections. That was the day I felt the weight of authority shift to me, while driving him around so he could talk privately about his memories and his moments of bitterness, which burst like bubbles as he described them. It's a hard day, and for a while you wear it like an ill-fitting jacket, the day the offer of membership to the terrible club is first extended.

In the late 1970s, on an airplane headed for Asia, my father happened to be seated next to Major Michael Crichton-Stuart, who at that time was hereditary keeper of Falkland Palace, in Fife, Scotland. They began talking, and after learning the major's occupation and where he lived, my dad mentioned that he thought he had Scottish ancestry but had never had it researched. Major Crichton-Stuart said he believed that my father might well have Scottish blood and that his ancestors may in fact have come from the exact area where the major lived, in the Kingdom of Fife, and more specifically the countryside around Strathmiglo and Falkland. There were ancient streets in Strathmiglo that contained the Cash name: Cash Easter, Cash Wester, Cash Feus, as well as a Cash mill and farm. Inspired by that chance conversation, my father became determined to find out more about his lineage, and he had our family tree traced back to the twelfth century. He learned that the Cash name did indeed originate in Fife, with Ada, half-sister of King Malcolm IV. She married Duncan, earl of Fife, and was given a land dowry of what is now Strathmiglo and the surrounding area, and the Falkland Forest, which comprised nine thousand acres in the year 1160. Ada and Duncan built a castle in the area, which has long since vanished, but our family roots and our visceral and spiritual connection to this area of Scotland run deep. My father developed a profound love and deep interest and passion for this part of Fife, and in 1981 he filmed a television special at Falkland Palace, where he reveled in the Scottish connection.

In 1998, I visited Falkland myself for the first time. Ninian Crichton-Stuart, son of Major Crichton-Stuart and the current laird, was kind enough to show John and me around the palace. We were completely overwhelmed and thrilled with the beauty and history, not only of the palace itself but of the entirety of Falkland and its environs, and we were deeply proud of my own connection to this beautiful place, however lost in ancient history those ties might be. The local newspaper even took our photo in front of the palace and featured us in the following day's edition.

In December 2003, twenty-two years after my father filmed that television special at the palace, and a few weeks after the Oslo concert, I returned to Scotland. I had been invited to perform at the BBC's Hogmanay show that New Year's Eve, and I came to Glasgow for rehearsals several days early with a heavy heart. I planned a free day in my schedule before arriving, because I knew I wanted to make the trip from Glasgow to Fife to honor my father and our Scottish ancestry, to see the palace and the towns of Falkland and

Strathmiglo again, and to find comfort in being in a place my father loved so very much. I think that on some level I also secretly hoped I would actually find *him* in Scotland as well. Carrie had accompanied me, and we set out from Glasgow by car early on the icy morning of December 28 to make the drive to Fife.

On our arrival in Falkland late in the morning, we were disappointed to find that the palace was closed for the holiday week. Just about everything was closed down, in fact, except for the little restaurant at the top of the hill, where we had a ploughman's lunch of bread, cheese, and pickles—a more satisfying meal than one offered by any four-star restaurant. After eating, we wandered next door to look in the window of the Old Violin Shop. Almost immediately my eye was caught by a beautiful old teapot, which was nearly identical to one I had inherited from June after her death the previous May. It was a squat, cream-colored porcelain vessel with a delicate pattern of pink and gold flowers and flourishes around its middle. I wanted it badly, but the shop, like all the others in town, was closed. I then noticed a note pinned to the door saying that if assistance was needed, to call a certain number. After several tries, I reached a very polite gentleman who said he was just finishing his lunch but promised to come shortly to let us in. Carrie and I waited in the car, as the weather was turning quite bitter. A few minutes later Bob Beveridge, the owner, appeared and invited us inside. After he carefully retrieved the teapot from the window, I began looking around at the instruments, books, china, paintings, and other collectibles. As Carrie and I began exclaiming to each other about the wondrous collection he had assembled, Bob noted our American accents and inquired if we had come to research our Scottish roots. I told him that I already knew the origin of my Scottish ancestry, and I was merely visiting the place my family name originated.

"Like Johnny Cash?" he asked, in a friendly manner, after asking my surname.

I hesitated, as I seldom told strangers who my father was, but I felt an impulse to confide in him.

"Yes, like Johnny Cash. He was my father," I said quietly.

His eyes widened. "I have something to show you," he said, and left the room.

He came back with a photograph of himself with my father, taken during the filming of the television special. He then began telling me the story of my father's visit.

My father liked to sit on a small cement post in front of the palace, Bob recalled, and to gaze at the square. All the townspeople came to speak to him, and he was unfailingly gracious and kind, which drew even more of the locals to him. He remembered that, one day, my father was in his car and came upon a boy whose bicycle had broken down in the road, so he picked him up and took him home. This boy, Bob explained, was now a man in his thirties, lived around the corner, and still loved to tell the story of the day he was driven home by Johnny Cash. Bob knew about my dad's fateful meeting with Major Crichton-Stuart on the plane to Asia, and he told me more stories of those few days, twenty-two years earlier, when Johnny Cash, along with a film crew and his special musical guest, Andy Williams, had taken over the town of Falkland, and how the people had loved him and he had loved them back.

I stood in the Old Violin Shop with tears running down my face, my wide-eyed teenage daughter standing next to me. It was a moment out of ordinary time, a serendipitous meeting I knew I had come halfway around the world to make, propelled by love, grief, and mysterious, ancient connections.

There is no place on earth like Fife. There is no town like Falkland, and no structure like its palace. The stones resonate with centuries of royal and familial history, tragedies and triumphs, beauty, glory, and tradition. It is a place that has a spirit large enough to contain the past, the present, and the future all at once. The original dowry given to Ada, so many centuries ago, stated that the land was given *in liberum maritagium*, or frank marriage; in other words, for the benefit of her heirs. Spiritually, I had claimed my inheritance.

It didn't surprise me that I had gone to Falkland searching for the part of my father that would always exist, and found a kind gentleman with a photograph of him standing near the very spot where I now stood. It didn't surprise me that love and family ties permeated even the stones in the streets of this magical place, and that it was home to those who loved it, whether they resided there or not.

It had nearly frightened, but hadn't surprised, me how much my father was there the night of the Oslo prison concert. Of course he never heard it, never knew it took place, never saw the yellow lights that dropped like giant egg yolks on the cobblestones, never walked through the icy fog into a roomful of facsimiles of himself. And yet there he was, liberated from the small pins of hurt and regret that had stayed lodged in his heart, released from the wrecked cars, the ravaged old/young body, and the grown children who needed assurance in the most unlikely places. I think he was finally comfortable with the tears at Oslo prison, and at Falkland Palace, perhaps even reveled in them with love and permanent detachment, as a man can do when he knows he is not responsible anymore.

On November 27, 2007, I got up at five a.m. and took a shower. After dressing in a blue-and-white-striped Comme des Garçons man-style shirt, black trousers, and black satin ballet slippers, I went down to the kitchen, where John, Chelsea, and my sister Tara were waiting for me with controlled, unnaturally calm expressions and superficial cheeriness. I was having none of it and instead started singing softly, "If I only had a brain . . ."

"Mom, STOP!" my daughter said with annoyance.

I asked my sister to take my picture with my cell phone. I look at that photo today and can't believe how bad I looked.

We got in the car and drove up the West Side Highway to Columbia Presbyterian Hospital at the northern tip of Manhattan. I put my headphones on for part of the drive so I could listen to my "preparation for surgery" relaxation tape, which Nolan Baer, a talented hypnotherapist and friend, had made for me. After checking into the hospital, I was sent to a holding room on another floor, which reminded me of a backstage greenroom but with a lot of scary equipment and no refreshments. As my small entourage stepped through the door, a woman seated at a nearby desk warned crankily, "Only two other people."

I looked at my sister and my daughter. "Both of you go upstairs,"

I said. "It will be easier if just John is here." We hugged quickly and they left.

As I put on a hospital gown, I felt my stomach begin to churn and asked for a Valium. I went to the bathroom, twice, but nothing was happening. Back in the holding room I perched on a gurney in my personal little cubicle—one of several little cubicles arranged in a semicircle around a lot of carts and shelves and busy nurses in the center of the room—and took my husband's hand. After a few minutes, a tiny, lovely dark-haired nurse came to officially check me in. She said hello and looked at my chart. Although she knew full well why I was there, she asked sweetly, "And what are you here for?"

"Liposuction," I replied without a smile.

Her eyes grew wide, and she froze. I could see her mentally running through the list of possible consequences of her misunderstanding: *disciplinary board hearings, lawsuits, job loss . . .*

"Stop torturing her," my husband said gently.

"I'm here for brain surgery," I said and this time smiled.

"Whew," she said, smiling in return. "Okay. Can you explain it? Can you tell me exactly what kind of brain surgery?" she asked, pen poised above my chart.

She certainly didn't need me to explain it, but there must have been a check to mark beside a notation that read "Patient fully understands nature of procedure." I mused for a moment. Brain surgery covers a wide range of possible events, from the drama of snipping giant aneurysms to brain mapping of a conscious patient for epilepsy, from the minor surgery of drilling tiny holes and placing shunts to relieve spinal fluid to—to my case.

"I'm having a decompression craniectomy and laminectomy for Chiari 1 and syringomyelia," I said in a self-confident rush, having researched these terms so thoroughly over the past three months that they now rolled off my tongue as easily as "verse, chorus, bridge." In other words, a brain surgeon was going to take a Midas Rex drill, saw open the back of my head, remove a credit card–sized portion of my skull, cut through the lining of my brain, break my top verte-bra, free my entrapped cerebellum and release the dam of spinal fluid, close the hole in my skull with a Gore-Tex patch, and then staple my head together, straight down the back, like a big zipper.

I somehow always knew that I would have brain surgery. From childhood, it seemed like a familiar experience, and something that didn't unduly frighten me. (That's not entirely true—it frightened me terribly, but it didn't seem out of the realm of normal potential life experiences.) I am not sure why, but I do know that when I was advised by five different neurosurgeons to have brain surgery, and not to take too long in getting it done, it seemed like a foregone conclusion, a foretold event.

I had had debilitating headaches for twelve years prior to my diagnosis. My neurologist was a migraine specialist and saw every-thing through the lens of his own specialty, as many doctors do. First he told me I had migraines. Then, when some of the headaches didn't follow a predictable model, he said I had "atypical" migraines. Then, when the atypical migraines became part of a laundry list of other symptoms that were difficult to parse, he told me I had mi-graines complicated by hormonal changes and stress, the catchall diagnosis for women in middle age. I became desperate for help. The headaches were happening every day. I had to quit yoga, which I had done for over a decade and which I loved, because my spine hurt and my neck was in constant spasm. I had been hit by a couple of "thunderclap" headaches in yoga class—which feel like being struck by lightning, hence the name—and I was leery of going back. I was also losing my stamina. I had been a workhorse; no schedule had ever been too daunting for me, but I was beginning to tire after just a single flight or a single show, something that had never happened before, even with the headaches. I had a few MRIs and was told there was nothing significant or troubling.

By the summer of 2007, I was in constant pain, had suffered a series of high fevers and infections, and was constantly exhausted. In August I decided to change neurologists, and went to see Dr. Norman Latov at Cornell. Within two weeks, after a series of new scans, he diagnosed me .

"I can't help you with this, and there are only a few neurosurgeons in the city who I would trust with this," he said as he began to write out referrals.

"Neurosurgeons? Is it a tumor?" I asked. I felt very calm, even relieved.

"No, not at all," he said. Then he told me he had seen only two people with my condition in his professional life, but he was confident I could get better.

"What did he say?" John asked when I called him after leaving the office.

"My cerebellum is too low, and it's crushing my brain stem," I told him, using this new vocabulary with unexpected confidence. "It's creating a dam. I have only a trickle of spinal fluid going into my head, and I have a swelling—something called a syrinx—in my spine, from the pressure of the fluid not being able to get up into my brain." I paused. "How do you feel about brain surgery?" I was trying to be casual, so I wouldn't upset John unduly, and also to inure myself against the shock by saying it aloud.

John, as is his nature, took this news calmly and reasonably, and immediately tracked down the top five neurosurgeons in the country.

We sent my scans around the country and arranged phone consultations with a doctor at Johns Hopkins, one at UCLA, and the head of neurosurgery at the University of Wisconsin (a colleague of John's brother-in-law), and had appointments with two others in New York City. All five said the same thing, basically, although one put it particularly succinctly: "That little trickle of fluid you have in your head? That's what's keeping you alive."

We eventually chose Dr. Guy McKhann II—a kind young neurosurgeon and himself the son of the neurologist we had consulted with at Johns Hopkins—at Columbia Presbyterian to do the surgery that had been prescribed. He encouraged me to prepare myself mentally, as it was going to be a tough ordeal. That was an understatement.

The hardest part of the three months between my diagnosis and the surgery was the time I woke in the middle of the night to find John leaning over me, his tears falling on my face. He was the most perfect patient advocate anyone could hope for. He was a rock and a defender and a guide, and only that one night, when he thought I was asleep, did it ever become too much for him.

Dr. McKhann, who would soon be making his way into my head, now approached me with a team of even younger doctors flanking him on either side. "How are you doing?" he asked as genially as the intake nurse had.

"Just great," I replied. "But how did *you* sleep last night?" I asked anxiously, trying to put aside visions of a sleepy, shaky neurosurgeon doing any of the procedures I had been imagining so obsessively.

"Perfect," he said.

"And have you read Jimmy Breslin's book on brain surgery?" I asked. (I had devoured a few books about neurosurgery in preparation for my own: the great novel *Saturday* by Ian McEwan, *When the Air Hits Your Brain* by Frank Vertosick, and Jimmy Breslin's account of his surgery for a dangerous aneurysm, *I Want to Thank My Brain for Remembering Me*. Breslin's account was written in his characteristic old-school newspaperman's clipped tones, and I had found it both charming and compelling.)

Dr. McKhann looked bemused. "No, should I?"

"Stop it," John said again gently.

My anesthesiologist, Dr. Eric Heyer, sauntered up. I suspected—and hoped—that he had a wicked sense of humor, which I thought I had glimpsed in our consultations up to this point. I had total confidence in his ability to keep me deeply unconscious—"below the level at which the brain can imprint memory"—and immobile during surgery, but I was also counting on his wit to help me get through the next half hour, while I was still awake and anxious. I looked at him eagerly.

"Have they given you the Valium yet?" he asked.

"No," I said, perhaps a bit more forlornly than I intended.

He stepped over to the nurse's station and found one for me and held it out in his palm. I took it and swallowed it gratefully.

"Okay!" he said as jauntily as if we were headed for a pleasant Sunday drive in the country. "Let's go!"

"I was hoping it would have time to work first," I grumbled faintly as I got off the gurney.

Dr. McKhann said he would see me later. I hugged John quickly—refusing to give space for any excess melodrama to arise—and told Dr. Heyer I didn't want to be wheeled into the operating room. I explained that I would be more frightened if I didn't step into it under my own steam.

"Fine with me," he said, and Dr. Heyer and I walked to the operating room together. Just as we pushed through the big double doors, he leaned over and whispered to me, "I've done this twice before, and it turned out well both times!"

I entered laughing, took a wary look at the array of computers they were going to hook up to my brain, and climbed up onto the table. A very young resident, one of the team who would be rearranging the map of my brain, was beside the table, wearing Buddhist mala beads around his neck. He smiled at me. I suddenly felt more relaxed. Then an adorable senior resident in a Russian skullcap stuck a needle in my arm, and just when I was about to start flirting with him, I drifted into unconsciousness and the day went by.

Six hours later, the first words I heard were Dr. McKhann's, asking me if I knew where I was. I opened my eyes. I was still in the OR, but the color of the walls was similar to that of my kitchen.

"I'm in my kitchen," I mumbled. I heard him laugh.

"No, you're not in your kitchen," he said. I closed my eyes.

"Yes I am," I insisted drowsily.

Then I saw John's smiling face hovering over me, and I smiled back as reassuringly as I could manage, to let him know I wasn't brain-damaged and that he could stop worrying. When I awoke again, I was in the neurological ICU and had the most unbelievable headache, one that made the pain of childbirth seem like a routine dental cleaning. That particular headache would last, I would soon discover, for a few months.

I was pumped so full of steroids and morphine that first week that I recall very little in specific detail. I do remember the pain. I also remember that my special black tea, which I had brought from home, tasted completely different than it normally did, and I remember how frustrated I was that something as simple and familiar as a cup of tea didn't provide the usual comfort and satisfaction. I remember walking for the first time, two days after the surgery, and the effort it required to remember how to step up a single stair. John practiced with me. "First you put one foot on the stair," he urged, "then you lift your body and then the other foot . . ."—instructions that seemed so hopelessly confusing that I struggled to understand the sequence. "Why can't you do this?" John asked calmly, staring at me. There was no fear in his tone of voice that I might be damaged, no frustration, just a simple question that I could ask myself: "Why can't I do this?" Until I could.

I remember the residents, who checked in on me several times a day, and how sweet they were, particularly the one wearing the mala beads. He had a special gift for healing just with his presence. I remember the pain service doctor, who carried a full syringe of morphine in his pocket and whom I actually pulled down to me and kissed once, in utter gratitude. (He blushed but seemed flattered.) The photos my sister took during my hospital stay reveal that I had a spectacular view of the Hudson River from my room in the McKeen Pavilion, but really, it was wasted on me. I remember crying when I was alone at night, while watching Tom Cruise in *Mission: Impossible*. I remember eight-year-old Jake coming to visit, and trying to test him on his spelling as he lay next to me in the hospital bed. *"Mom!"* he reprimanded me, after a couple of words. "You're falling asleep!"

Six days later, they sent me home. John didn't tell Jake he was bringing me home that day. He got me settled in bed, and then brought Jake into the bedroom to surprise him. His little face melted with relief when he saw me and tears filled his eyes. I suddenly realized the depth of the stress and worry he had been carrying, and keeping to himself. He climbed onto the bed and I hugged him tightly.

I had nineteen staples up the back of my head. I learned there was a community of people who had my condition and had gone through the same surgery, who called themselves zipperheads. I was mildly amused, and enjoyed referring to myself that way on occasion, but I adamantly refused to join any community that identified itself by an illness. The idea of becoming a spokesperson for this condition, which I was asked to do before the staples were even out of my head, was appalling to me, and entirely against my nature and sense of privacy—I was not inclined to trade publicly on anything relating to my health or my body, even, unfortunately, in the service of others who suffered with the same disease. The recovery was hard, harder than I imagined. I think I expected just to have headaches, but that kind of surgery is a total body event. I was traumatized, weak, and everything hurt—not just my head. Before the surgery, I foolishly thought in three months I would be better, so I had planned to resume performing, and the first dates on the calendar were in mid-March. I went to Florida to play a show, and the flight alone set me back by weeks. I regrouped. This was just going to take a lot longer than I had anticipated, and I would readjust my planned trajectory back to health.

My friends, particularly my girlfriends, were phenomenal. Every day for the first few weeks, someone would come by to sit and watch a Bette Davis movie with me, or drop off a casserole for John and the kids, or just sit quietly next to me on the bed when I was too miserable to talk or listen. Chantal Bacon, my next-door neighbor and one of my dearest friends, visited many times just to make tea for me, as she knew exactly how I liked it. She would brew a pot, arrange it on a tray, smile, and almost imperceptibly leave. My friends

Gael Towey and Stephen Doyle made applesauce for me a few times, and it became the only thing I wanted to eat. Stephen ferried it over to me on his bicycle. Chelsea went back and forth to Nashville, where she was living, to help with Jake and the house, and calm Carrie's nerves about me.

John read aloud to me Chekhov's "The Bet," and in my morphine haze the images and language became almost surreal, and wonderful. That was perhaps the best moment in my early recovery.

Because of the slow pace of recovery, I was frustrated and even despairing at times. I went deep into my pain, ascribing all kinds of portentous meaning to it. The changes in barometric pressure that accompanied an approaching storm laid me out on the sofa, immobile, with a crushing headache. They had broken my top vertebra during surgery, intentionally, so they could free up the trapped cerebellum, and my neck felt like a concrete brick. It hurt constantly. My left ear developed overly acute hearing, and I found that I couldn't bear not only noise but any music with lyrics—the words seemed too complicated, and irritating. I listened to classical music in those first few months, and nothing else. Mostly I wanted silence. I was enormously sensitive to sensory overload, and I stayed inside my house most of the time to avoid sounds of traffic and sirens, loud voices, and dogs barking. Sometimes I reversed words when I was talking, or replaced common words with others that weren't even close in meaning. My friends laughed when that happened and told me it was adorable, that I shouldn't worry about it.

In my self-pity I went so far as to convince myself that both my parents had somehow known I was going to have brain surgery and had decided to die before it happened so they wouldn't have to go through the agony of seeing their child undergo such a terrific ordeal. This little exercise in morbid narcissism allowed me to become furious with them, and feel justified. Then, at some point, that all dissipated and I was glad—more than glad, I was deeply relieved—that they weren't around to witness it, as I knew how much it would have taken out of both of them. My brother came up to New York from his home in Tennessee, and my sister from her home in Portland, Oregon, to offer comfort in lieu of our parents. I was grateful for that.

Today my face is no longer as round as a hubcap from steroids, and the initial egregious pain from the surgery has mercifully faded, but a kind of posttraumatic memory pain endures. On some days it is almost cripplingly awful and others barely noticeable, and I have grown used to my missing vertebra and the little ski jacket in my skull. I am still sensitive to too much sensory information and have given up taking the subway because the sound frequency of the trains is unbearable. A loud party can make me shaky and dizzy. But my most recent MRIs look fantastic. Dr. McKhann was so thrilled with the results, he said, that if he showed my MRI at a conference, he would be told that he performed unnecessary surgery, that there was no evidence of a Chiari. I don't see Dr. Heyer anymore, but he has been replaced by two other fantastic men—my pain specialist, Dr. Michael Weinberger, and my physical therapist, Evan Johnson—and a wonderful acupuncturist, Shellie Goldstein.

They are diligent, meticulous, and constantly encouraging. I use pain medication only on rare occasions, and my doctors all assure me that there is "no limit to how much I can still improve." I take this as gospel, on all levels, metaphoric and physical.

I'm glad I had brain surgery. My cerebellum was in a rogue location: It had done the geographical equivalent of starting in Vancouver and wandering down to Houston. The map had to be rearranged. But I don't recommend it as an elective adventure. I don't recommend it without the presence of my husband, who will call several of the top neurosurgeons in the country and compile all their opinions in a spiral notebook and then drive you to the hospital and make sure you see his face as soon as you are remotely conscious and help you learn to walk up one stair, and try to make the tea taste right, and take over the spelling words when you pass out, and read short stories to you, and show up again and again and again. And I don't recommend it unless the idea of brain surgery keeps resurfacing in the background noise of the foreshadowed knowledge of your own life. It's too big, and it takes a long time to explain it to yourself, not to mention to others. It scares the shit out of everyone. It requires a steely, aggressive sense of humor. There are too many aftershocks in the way of nightmares and pain. But if it *is* a foregone conclusion in your life, I highly recommend Jimmy Breslin's book, a good night's sleep, the score from *The Wizard of Oz*, a relaxation tape, Chekhov and morphine, and a decent cup of tea.

Recently someone sent me an issue of *Guitar Player* magazine to show me an old photograph taken in London in 1985 on the set of a television show. It featured a group of musicians sitting in a circle with their instruments. There was Carl Perkins, and there were George Harrison and Eric Clapton, Dave Edmunds and Ringo Starr. Right at the center was a young woman with spiked hair and knee-high leather boots, holding a tambourine: me. I was thirty years old. I was the token woman on this show, a fact the producers hadn't bothered to disguise when they invited me to participate. I didn't care. I stepped off the plane and went straight to rehearsal and walked into that crowded studio and into another life, as far as I was concerned. I don't think I ever told my parents I was going to do this show, and I don't think I told them after the fact, either. I don't know if they ever saw it. I went to George Harrison's house for dinner that night with all the guys and listened to them play old rockabilly and blues songs for hours. I was completely exhausted from the flight and a full day of work and from pretending that I had total confidence in my right to be there. But pretending I had the confidence made it easier for me to generate a little of the genuine article, and a moment I later had with George helped in that respect tremendously.

The following night, as I left the television stage after my song, I saw George standing in the wings, waiting to go on. He was clapping for me, but I shook my head and said despondently, "It wasn't as good as rehearsal." "It's *never* as good as rehearsal," he replied, and I saw then that he was nervous. *George Harrison was nervous about appearing on a television show and performing a song.* I thought about that so many years later, when I attended the memorial for him in Strawberry Fields in Central Park the first weekend of December 2001, a few days after he died of lung cancer. He didn't take his Beatles baggage to the guest spot on the Carl Perkins television show, but was just in the moment, wanting to be good, like the rest of us.

I have a friend who vacations for a month on Fisher Island every summer, another who goes to Maine for August, several who enjoy many leisurely weeks on the Vineyard upstate, and quite a few who are unreachable from June to Labor Day. I relish their summer vacation stories; I even obsess over them. I need all the details. (What was the house like? No, what was it like *exactly*? How far from the beach in feet and inches? What did you grill? How did you find a babysitter up there? What did you do? *Eat? Play?*)

I am not one of those people. Because every June, as soon as my son goes to summer camp, I leave Manhattan and go to work on the road. I tour with a full band and crew, or as part of an acoustic trio, but often it is just John and me out there doing our folk-rock George and Gracie show. Once, when we had a day off in Anchorage and drove up on the mountain that overlooks the Cook Inlet to watch the most spectacular sunset I've ever seen, I got lulled into thinking that we were on a kind of vacation. And I allowed myself to get a little happy. Then, two days later, comes a 4 a.m. call for a 6:30 plane, which flies three and a half hours to get to an airport bus to take us to a rental car for a four-and-a-half-hour drive into some godforsaken wilderness where some genius has had the foresight to book a folk festival, which I play that very night and which pays a significant chunk of my New York state taxes for the coming year (which means it is an appearance I cannot afford to turn down), reminding me that I am most definitely not on vacation, that I am, in fact, in a kind of bizarre rolling parallel universe that only those who have done summer tours can truly appreciate.

The road can be numbing, though I prefer driving to flying, as I seem to have a thing about flight attendants, having developed over the years a hypersensitivity to attitude at high altitudes. I have been in planes that have been struck by lightning, surrounded by tornadoes, diverted to new and even more miserably inconvenient destinations; planes whose landing gear failed to descend, engines conked out, wings clipped the ground and spewed rivets across the runway, takeoffs and landings have been aborted in snow and ice storms and violent winds and rain; planes that dropped so fast and so far that people literally hit the ceiling; and once, on a nearly empty late-night flight into Nashville, the pilot sent an attendant back just after landing to ask me if I knew where Gate 4 was, since he thought I had probably landed at this particular airport more than he had. And I had.

But a wonderful audience on an inspired night in a beautiful setting is like nothing else on earth. There is almost always that moment onstage when I feel guilty for complaining, because the audience is just so great and so responsive, and I realize that they really did come to see me, and I feel as if I might actually have a larger purpose in the world. I do it, ultimately, because I love it.

Once, in Montana, I drove by a hot springs resort set at the base of a magnificent mountain, in the midst of a spectacular valley. The landscape was beyond imagination: dramatic peaks and wide meadows and a river that shone from bank to bank and twisted through the valley from end to end. A convention of scientists had gathered at the resort, and a big white tent had been set up on the lawn, full of people milling about and having drinks. Outside the tent, some fifty yards away, sat a man in white shirtsleeves and khakis perched on a boulder at the foot of a little hillock, reading some papers in his left hand and nervously drumming his fingers on his leg with his right hand as he mouthed words silently to himself. I assumed he was the next speaker at the convention and was rehearsing his speech. I looked at the view behind and around him—the mountains, the valley, the Yellowstone River—and suddenly thought to myself, *It's me. That's me.* Obsessing over the details, how I will sound and appear, working it out, preparing, while all around me was a vast expanse of beauty and natural magnificence, unnoticed. It took me a long time to begin to let go, to quiet the critical voices, to stop editing. Performing is energy exchange. Sometimes it's hard work, priming the pump, finding where the audience's connectors are, and sometimes I just have to get out of my own way so they can take me on a ride. The ephemeral nature of live performance is the part I love most—it's a monk's sand painting, carefully constructed, then wiped away in an instant.

. . . . .

I have built my career with my eyes half closed and both parents held at arm's length, for opposite reasons: My father was too close to what I wanted to do; my mother too distant.

My mother led with her feelings. She made business decisions based on how she felt about someone, she hired lawyers because they seemed nice, she personalized what was not personal and was held captive by her own projections, based on feelings that were many times unfounded in reality. She also revealed her secrets and deepest pain to those who were not trustworthy, because she was easily taken in by gratuitous flattery and the whiff of obsequiousness. She could never properly discern character behind polished falsity. Conversely, she withheld her own truth from those who might have helped her if there was an appearance of detachment, or calculated logic and reason, in the person in question. Sometimes that person in question was me. She was half Sicilian, and she was incredibly sensitive and emotionally volatile. She felt deeply and didn't let go easily. She found her own internal emotional landscape bewildering and overwhelming much of the time. It was so much for her to navigate. To me, it seemed like too much work, a ruinous distraction from the creative life, and an exhausting and unpredictable way to live. I saw I had a choice. My heart ached for her, a prisoner of so many feelings, so unbounded by reason, but I lived in reaction to her much of the time.

My father, in many ways, also led with his feelings, but he was of a more stoic, enigmatic nature, and much of the time we didn't know what he was feeling until long after the fact, if ever. More to the point, he was a transcendent artist, which gave form and context and rhythm to those feelings, and the world was all the better for it. Living inside himself wasn't easy—in fact, it was almost impossible for him to stay inside the terms of physical life and the limits of the body and mind, and he tested those limits many times, in many ways. But he did have a forum for his emotional life, the vastness of it, the grandeur and the pain. My mother did not have such a vast forum, although the forum she did have—her garden and her many domestic arts—was ultimately her salvation and a source of great beauty. Both were suited to the types of lives they created for themselves. That sounds obvious, but I think it was providential. I know plenty of people who are *not* suited to the lives they create for themselves.

To engage either of them in the seeding of my future, and the understanding of myself as an artist, would have been inconceivable tasks for me, as it would have meant analyzing them, refuting them, rebelling against them, explaining myself, seeking solace, or submitting. So I did the only thing left to me: I withdrew.

My father accepted this quietly. I imagine he understood, even though I know there were times that it hurt him that I didn't ask for his advice or allow him into the inner workings of my plans. My mother accepted my ambition reluctantly and with a lot of anxiety, and with some judgments about the way I dressed or conducted myself, which were fair enough. I wore white pumps with a black suit on a big, splashy television show, when I should have been wearing an evening gown. I colored my hair purple. I abandoned Catholicism, making moot her most careful maternal training. I had no

problem telling people to go fuck themselves when I felt it was warranted, even though I was not abrasive by nature and in fact was
brought up to be a people-pleaser, a loathsome inclination. I didn't
suffer fools gladly, even when I was one myself. I also recklessly
walked along a well-worn familial path at the edge of an abyss, by
using drugs in my twenties. Fortunately, I didn't have whatever it is
in the brain chemistry that creates addiction and I stopped abruptly
and forever when it became clear that it was a course of greatly di-
minishing returns. Such breaches of conduct and form were almost
more than my mother could bear. Looking back, I now see that some
are almost more than I can bear, too.

But out of various forms of personal catastrophe comes art, if
you're lucky. And I have been lucky. I have also been driven by a
deep love and obsession with language, poetry, and melody. I had
first wanted to be a writer, in a quiet room, setting depth charges of
emotion in the outside world, where my readers would know me
only by my language. Then I decided I wanted to be a songwriter,
writing not for myself but for other voices who would be the vehicles
for the songs I created. Then, despite myself, I began performing my
own songs, which rattled me to the core. It took me a long time to
grow into an ambition for what I had already committed myself to
doing, but I knew I could be good at it if I put my mind to it. So I put
my mind to it.


We all need art and music like we need blood and oxygen. The more
exploitative, numbing, and assaulting popular culture becomes, the

more we need the truth of a beautifully phrased song, dredged from a real person's depth of experience, delivered in an honest voice; the more we need the simplicity of paint on canvas, or the arc of a lonely body in the air, or the photographer's unflinching eye. Art, in the larger sense, is the lifeline to which I cling in a confusing, unfair, sometimes dehumanizing world. In my childhood, the nuns and priests insisted, sometimes in a shrill and punitive tone, that religion was where God resided and where I might find transcendence. I was afraid they were correct for so many years, and that I was the one at fault for not being able to navigate the circuitry of dogma and ritual. For me, it turned out to be a decoy, a mirage framed in sound and fury. Art and music have proven to be more expansive, more forgiving, and more immediately alive. For me, art is a more trustworthy expression of God than religion.

The first good song I ever wrote took me the better part of a day, with no interruptions. I lay on the floor of Renate Damm's apartment in Munich in 1978 and didn't lift my head, except to quickly eat something or go to the bathroom, until it was finished. It was called "This Has Happened Before." It's a young woman's song, tentative and too self-referential, too navel-gazing, but not to an extreme that would make you squirm. It's well constructed, painstaking even, and I can hear the hard work in it. I was very proud when I finished that song, and it was the first time I felt like a real songwriter. I was twenty years old.

In the summer of 1994, I was in Paris, alone, finishing my book of short stories. On a beautiful late afternoon, I was walking toward the Seine from the Panthéon when, wafting out of the open door of a record shop, I heard a song by Guy Clark, who was a distant hero when I first began to write, then a genial mentor and friend, along with Rodney, when I lived in Nashville. I stopped in the street to listen to the song, and then went inside the store. There were racks and racks of vinyl records, all, it seemed, by American folk and roots musicians. I was ecstatic. I started flipping through the racks and came upon several of my own records.

At that moment the owner came up to me and said with authority, as he pointed to *Rhythm and Romance,* "No, no, no. This one is not good." He flipped through a couple more albums and pulled out *King's Record Shop.* "THIS one. This is a great record."

I looked at him and smiled. He didn't make the connection.

Shyly, I said, "It's me." He still didn't understand. I raised the album next to my face. *"C'est moi.* It's me."

"Oh my God!" he gasped, and we both laughed. We retired to a nearby café and drank a bottle of red wine together and talked about music.

It's me. They are all me, the good and the bad.

I want to know what lives behind language; I am both limited and ennobled by words and rhyme. The songs have been an attempt to discover the mysteries. In a more proscribed way, my life is entirely contained in my songs, even the ones I wrote in other voices and characters ("Last Stop Before Home," "The Good Intent"), and even the ones I wrote to try (unsuccessfully) to get some big country artist to record so I could get myself out of debt ("Closer Than I Appear").

Sometimes songs are indeed postcards from the future, and are not written out of prescience as much as time travel. Thornton Wilder said, "It is only in appearance that time is a river. It is rather a vast landscape and it is the eye of the beholder that moves." In songwriting, I have found my attention to wander both forward and backward on that continuum. But with or without prescience, considering only the hard-earned craftsmanship of songwriting, as I get older I have found the quality of my attention to be more important, and more rewarding, than the initial inspiration. This maturation in songwriting has proven surprisingly satisfying. Thirty years ago I would have said that the bursts of inspiration, and the ecstatic flood of feeling that came with them, were an emotionally superior experience, preferable to the watchmaker's concentration required for the detail work of refining, editing, and polishing. But the reverse is proving to be true. Like everything else, given enough time and the long perspective, the opposite of those things that we think define us slowly becomes equally valid and sometimes more potent. I have learned to be steady in my course of love, or fear, or loneliness, rather than impulsive in its wasting, either lyrically or emotionally. The discipline I began to refine after I dreamed of Art during *King's Record Shop* has paid off immeasurably, and provided context for my entire life.

. . . . .

Paradoxically, I discovered an unexpected sense of mastery and of musical shelter through releasing my first album of covers, *The List*, in 2009. The list of songs my dad had given me on a tour bus rolling through the South in 1973, right after I graduated from high school, when he was afraid I lacked half the essential knowledge I needed to become a roots musician (he knew I knew my Lennon and McCartney and my Neil Young, but not Woody Guthrie or Jimmie Rodgers), became the source material for an understanding of the fullness of my own legacy. John and I carefully chose an album's worth of songs from that list and we brought everything we knew, both together and separately, about this music, from decades of love and study, to *The List*. I had saved the list Dad made me in a box of letters for all these years, never thinking I would record any of those songs—I was a songwriter, separately and defiantly—but after losing my parents, and after the brain surgery, some ideas that had been on the periphery of my dreams began to take sharp and urgent focus, and making a record of these songs that were so clearly part of Dad's musical genealogy, and therefore my own, became a primary goal. It was a 180-degree turn; the idea of stepping into a body of work outlined for me by Dad had always been far too complicated for me to consider. I had done an exhausting dance with his legacy for my entire life. Again, it was John who encouraged me. "It's time to step into this," he said. "It's your legacy, too." Again, he was right. It dawned on me during the recording that it was a record I wanted to make for my children as much as for myself or the honor of my ancestors. Traditions can take root out of the dormant impulses of one's own soul, if they are powerful enough, whether we acknowledge them or not. I finally had the wisdom and the grace not only to acknowledge but to revere them and embody them with real joy.

*The List* represents a kind of resolution, of so many seemingly disparate but intimately related themes and struggles in my life, both musical and personal. I had so much fear of exploiting my father, and not doing things on my own, but it was more than that. He cast an obviously large shadow, and it was hard for me to find my own place outside of it, or to be comfortable when the shadow was the first thing people noticed about my life or my work. Dad himself understood my struggle and gave me a lot of room, and a lot of purely parental approval. But the times I did approach the legacy that the list represented, his excitement was unbounded. When "Tennessee Flat-Top Box" became a number one record for me, he was delirious with happiness. In the last few months of his life, I enthusiastically sang all the old Carter Family songs to him when he rested in the afternoons, and I could see it was a tremendous solace, not only because of the songs themselves, but because he saw that I was beginning to say yes. I wish he had been alive to hear *The List*, and to see me say yes to all of it, and more than that, to revel in it as if it were a secret passed from parent to child, and a key to a particular familial mystery. Now it's Chelsea's turn, and John and I wouldn't be surprised if Jake followed as well, as the next generation of musicians and songwriters in our family to do their own dance with their parents and grandparents, and to listen for the secrets.

In the fullness of that legacy, I am still first and foremost a songwriter. The curatorial work and the deliberate attention on my voice rather than my words, which happened with *The List*, has only added to my sense of honor as a songwriter and respect for the art and discipline.

I have a fear that I have a personal quota, bestowed at birth, of first-rate songs allotted to me, and I worry, after every new song I write, that I have finally reached that magic number. So, inevitably, mixed with the satisfaction of accomplishment is anxiety and sadness that this might be the end. The uncertainty is vexing, but it keeps me humble. I am always a beginner, again and again. I work, even when I worry.

I sing to the six percent, and they are me. I am not a pane of glass. There is light and it is always available. Much of it comes through music; at least half. And it turns out that a lonely road is a bodyguard.

# ACKNOWLEDGMENTS

I would not have written this book without the encouragement and faith of my editor, Rick Kot. Thank you, Rick, for asking me to do this more than a decade ago. Many thanks also to Laura Tisdel, assistant to Rick Kot, and a wonderful and deeply organized woman, and to my fabulous and long-suffering agent, Merrilee Heifetz, at Writers House. Grateful acknowledgment, always, to the teams of dedicated people at Viking and Manhattan Records, and thank you also to Christian Oth and to Anita Merk.

Thank you to Danny Kahn, my manager, who has envisioned great things for me when I lacked imagination to see them for myself, and who has taken nearly every step I've taken since then with unfailing cheer.

I owe special thanks to my family, for allowing me to depict them from my own myopic perspective. It is incredibly generous, and I am very grateful to John, Kathy, Cindy, Tara, John Carter, Hannah, Caitlin, Chelsea, Carrie, and Jake, as well as Sylvia, Dick, and Rodney.

Gratitude goes to my friends who keep coming to see me perform, who come for tea, and who make great allowances for my schedule in our friendships, and especially the writers who offered me extra encouragement and support: Adriana Trigiani and Joe Henry for their inspiration and cheerleading, Kurt Andersen and Anne Kreamer for very particular advice, Wesley Stace and Bill Flanagan for the general love, and a special bow to George Kalogerakis, who keeps asking me to write things for him. Some of those things ended up in this book.

Tim McHenry, the director of programming at the Rubin Museum of Art, in Manhattan, has given me the great gift of allowing me to write and perform ten shows for the museum. It has offered me a unique forum to expand on a lot of musical ideas. Thank you, Tim.

I owe a tremendous debt to the superb musicians I have worked with over the years. I have learned so much from them. I have become not just a better musician, but a better person by being in the presence of those who use the available light of music as currency in the world. Many thanks to my vocal coaches, Marge Rivingston and William Riley.

I owe peripheral, but essential, thanks to the team of doctors who have taken care of me in the last few years, and who have brought me back to health: Dr. Norman Latov, Dr. Guy McKhann II, Dr. Eric Heyer, Dr. Lila Nachtigall, Dr. Barry Cohen, and Dr. Michael Weinberger. Thanks also to Dr. Jim Davis, who gave advice and referrals, and to Nolan Baer, Shellie Goldstein, and Evan Johnson for extraneous body and soul maintenance.

I wish I could thank my mother and father, for so many things I didn't have enough awareness or detachment to appreciate: thousands of acts of service and love, tolerance and support. I think of them every day.

Most especially, I thank John. He always pushes me to tell more, write it down, own it, share it. I'm so grateful that he does.

More to come.

# FRONTISPIECE CAPTIONS

Row 1: Johnny and Vivian Cash; Rosanne, age seven

Row 2: Johnny with Rosanne (top left), Cindy, and Kathy, circa
1959; Vivian holding Tara, with Kathy (right), Cindy (middle),
and Rosanne (left), circa 1962

Row 3: John Leventhal at home, 2009; Johnny Cash walks his
daughter down the aisle, 1995; Rosanne in performance under a full moon, Germany, 2008

Row 4: John and Rosanne, Guana Island, 2008; Rosanne's five
children at Caitlin's wedding, from left to right: Chelsea,
Jake, Caitlin, Carrie, and Hannah